SOUTHERN APPALACHIAN

Wildflowers

A Field Guide to Common Wildflowers of the Southern Appalachian Mountains, Including Great Smoky Mountains National Park, the Blue Ridge Parkway, and the Chattahoochee National Forest

by Barbara Medina and Victor Medina

FALCON®
GUILFORD, CONNECTICUT
AN IMPRINT OF THE GLOBE PEQUOT PRESS

A FALCON GUIDE ®

Text design: Sue Cary
Photo credits: All photos by Barbara Medina unless otherwise noted.
Illustrations: Elizabeth Medina Gray

Library of Congress Cataloging-in-Publication Data is available.

ISBN: 0-7627-1135-3

Printed in Korea
First Edition/First Printing

CAUTION

Ingesting plants or plant parts poses a potentially extreme health hazard and could result in sickness or even death. No one should attempt to use any wild plant for food or medicine without adequate training by a fully qualified professional. The authors, publisher, and all others associated with the production and distribution of this book assume no liability for the actions of the reader.

All participants in the recreational activities suggested by this book must assume responsibility for their own actions and safety. The information contained in this guidebook cannot replace sound judgment and good decision-making skills, which help reduce risk exposure; nor does the scope of this book allow for disclosure of all the potential hazards and risks involved in such activities.

Learn as much as possible about the recreational activities in which you participate, prepare for the unexpected, and be cautious. The reward will be a safer and more enjoyable experience.

DEDICATION

Dedicated with love to Elizabeth and Jennifer, who, carrying on the family tradition, accompanied us on many a joyful wildflower hunt. They remind us to see the world with the enthusiasm and ever curious eyes of a child, and for this we are grateful.

CKNOWLEDGMENTS

We would like to thank the national, state, county, and regional agencies of the Southern Appalachian Mountains who protect our parks, forests, and the environment. The staffs have provided maps, answered our questions, and been very helpful whenever we needed guidance. The National Parks Service and Forest Service as well as the state and county park and forest managers from Alabama, Georgia, North Carolina, Tennessee, Virginia, and West Virginia have been very supportive whether we contacted them by telephone, on the Internet, or at the various visitors or interpretive centers. Without their guidance this book would have not been possible. We've listed agency, park, and forest addresses, phone numbers, and Internet addresses at the end of this book.

We also thank our editor, Erin Turner, and copyeditor, Erika Serviss, for their hard work and attention to detail on this book.

We particularly want to thank Elizabeth Medina Gray for her wonderful line drawings and Brian Gray for his guidance of the drawing project and labeling of the drawings.

CONTENTS

PREFACE

Wildflowers, no matter how beautiful they may be, are different things to different people. The herbalist pursues them as food and medicine. The farmer, seeing them among the crops, may think of them as nothing more than pests. The wildflower enthusiast sees them as masterpieces of form and color. This book provides guidance for finding and identifying many of the common herbaceous plants and shrubs that contribute to the spectacular splashes of seasonal color in the Southern Appalachian Mountains.

Outside of the tropics, one would have to travel to parts of China to see a greater diversity of wildflowers than that found in the Southern Appalachians. In addition to plants that are native to North America and to this region, we find plants in these southern mountains with origins in Europe or Asia. This great plant diversity is attributable to a number of factors.

Early in the North American continent's history, massive glaciers extended down from the north, ending somewhere around Pennsylvania and Ohio. It is generally believed that these glaciers never reached as far south as the Southern Appalachian Mountains and as a result, northern plants were pushed further and further south. Also in these southern regions, plant development proceeded without interruption, unlike in the more northern parts of the continent, which were periodically under oceans or glaciers millions of years ago. Finally, when settlers began arriving in this region they brought with them, intentionally and unintentionally, the seeds of plants from other parts of the world. Added to all of this, the rich soil, abundant rainfall, and variety of temperature zones in the Southern Appalachian Mountains contributed to successful competition by alien plants. The end result is the great variety of plants we now find in this region.

Plants gathered from the wild have provided humans with food, medicine, clothing, and shelter for thousands of years. Yarrow was used as an herbal remedy during the Roman Empire. Native Americans as well as the early settlers relied on squawroot, blue cohosh, coltsfoot, and many other wild plants for their entire medicine cabinet, while Jerusalem artichoke, Indian cucumber, and all sorts of berries were part of the seasonal fare.

Although we describe some plants that have been used for food or medicine, and despite a long and illustrious history of the benefits derived from nature's bounty, we caution against the ingestion of wild plants by the enthusiastic wildflower dabbler. Eating the wrong plant can lead to serious discomfort or at worst, hazardous toxic effects.

The desire to dig up wild plants and transplant them to a home garden may sometimes seem overwhelming, especially if the coveted plants are merely one or two in a field of hundreds. But this destructive practice is among the factors that have contributed to creating a long list of vanishing and endangered plant species. The loss of orchids and trilliums is still a well-known problem in the southern mountains. When taken to extremes, commercial collection of wild plants can approach the methods and numbers of past experiences. In the 1880s hundreds of thousands of pounds of hepatica were harvested for commercial processors who claimed medicinal powers for the product. One hundred years later an estimated 100 tons of ginseng root taken from the wild were shipped to the Far East. Removal of just one plant by an individual can produce an unbelievable cumulative effect—if each visitor to Great Smoky Mountains National Park picked just one plant, there would be a loss of some 9 million plants each year in that location alone. Many of these plants can thrive only under the very special conditions in which we find them in the wild, so for most collectors, transplantation is doomed to failure. If this argument fails then we point out that picking and removing plant material is illegal on federal lands and in most state and county parks. For those wishing to try their hand at planting "wildflowers" in their gardens, there are a number of reputable nurseries supplying seeds and plants that have not been derived from those taken out of the wild.

Many states, through the agencies responsible for protecting the environment or managing state parks and forests, maintain inventories of wild plants. These agencies would welcome information on where and when the less common wildflowers have been found. Contact information for these agencies and parks is listed at the back of this book. Park staff can forward the information to the proper agency.

Common names for wildflowers were often assigned based on some assumed property of the plant, its shape, or local legend. As a result, one plant may have many common names, varying with the regions of the country where it is found. Fortunately there are usually one or two more well known common names for each wildflower that are used regionally. The ones common to the Southern Appalachians are the ones we use in this book, along with the more precise scientific names. Sometimes botanists do not agree on botanical names for wildflowers, so to try to achieve some consistency in names, we've used the nomenclature adopted by several of the better-known eastern wildflower guides that use the botanical nomenclature of *Gray's Manual of Botany,* eighth edition.

Wildflowers are not always exactly the same shade for the same flower all the time in every place. Some flowers naturally grow in more than one color or shade, or may even be multicolored; we will point these out in our plant descriptions. Because of a number of factors, the color of a flower may vary when viewed in the field or in photographs. These disparities most affect flowers that are in the pink-to-red or lavender-to-blue or purple color ranges. To help the viewer quickly find flowers in these color ranges, we have put those few flowers that are almost always red, orange, or blue into those color categories and put all others in a pink-to-purple color category.

Wildflowers come in a variety of sizes from several inches to less than one-quarter of an inch wide. Seeing the details of these flowers can best be achieved with a magnifying glass, and we recommend taking one along on woodland walks. Those prepared to get down on their knees to peer at these flowers through such a lens will be rewarded with a spectacular view of this world of complex and startling shapes and colors.

*I*NTRODUCTION

The Appalachians

The rocks of the Appalachians strongly indicate that this chain of mountains is one of the most ancient in North America. Scientists theorize that during a period ending about 1 billion years ago, a series of cataclysmic movements of the earth's crust led to the formation of the landmass of North America. Geologists believe the Appalachians themselves are the result of a further series of massive movements of the earth's crust in eastern North America, which took place as early as 500 million years ago, ending some 300 million years later. During this period of crust collisions and volcanic activity, these great mountain-building forces lifted and folded rock layers, in some places bringing to the surface rocks that were originally 10 miles under the earth. In more recent time on the geological clock, from about 2 million years ago and ending 10,000 years ago, much of the northern continent was covered with glaciers that advanced and receded over time. The erosive forces of ice, wind, and water modified and sculpted the land, producing the Appalachian chain of mountains we see today.

The geologic history of a land goes a long way towards determining the types of plants that eventually thrive there. The moisture content of soil and the acidity of water reaching plant roots vary with the physical and chemical nature of the soil. Water moves downhill and, everything else being equal, leaves the tops of hills and mountains drier than the bottomlands. Moderating this will be the percolating properties of the soil and bedrock. Coarse soil will allow moisture to drain out more quickly than in areas with fine soils, which may retain more moisture. Also, the porosity of the bedrock will govern whether more or less water will accumulate in the soil above. The weather at the top of a 5,000-foot mountain will be quite different than that in the valley below, at the same time of year and at the same latitudes, affecting the plant life within the same mountain group. All these factors are at work in the great range of the Appalachians.

The entire Appalachian chain extends for more than 2,000 miles from Alabama to Newfoundland. For the most part, it is a narrow system running parallel to the east coast of North America. In most places, this mountain group is rarely more than 100 miles wide. There are a number of mountain ranges within the Appalachians bearing their own well-known names. The Blue Ridge Mountains running from Georgia to Pennsylvania, the Great Smoky Mountains in North Carolina and Tennessee, the Pocono Mountains of Pennsylvania, the Berkshires of Massachusetts, and the Long Range Mountains of Newfoundland are just a few of the named mountains within the Appalachians.

The Southern Appalachians

Some of the most splendid geological features of eastern North America are found in the ancient 2,000-mile-long Appalachian Mountains. The Southern Appalachian part of this chain is also home to an incredible variety of plants unequaled anywhere else in North America. This book describes and provides color pictures for 295 plants found in these mountains. The Southern Appalachian region described here stretches from the southern Blue Ridge Mountains in Virginia to the southern mountains of West Virginia, through the Great Smoky Mountains in North Carolina and Tennessee, to the Chattahoochee National Forest in Georgia, and the terminus of the Appalachians in Alabama.

From the sea in the east to these Southern Appalachians in the west, the region can be divided into several distinct physical zones. At the easternmost point, the Coastal Plain rises from the ocean's continental shelf and extends over the land westward to meet the Piedmont Plateau at a point called the fall line. Moving westward from the fall line, this Piedmont Plateau is a hilly region no higher than 800 feet, and it extends north to south from New York to Alabama. The Blue Ridge region begins at the western edge of the Piedmont Plateau as a series of low hills in southern Pennsylvania but quickly stretches south to the mountains of Shenandoah National Park with heights of more than 4,000 feet. The slopes of the Blue Ridge are covered with many streams flowing either east or west. The mountain streams on the east side run into the Piedmont region and then run through tributaries of the Potomac and Rapahannock Rivers feeding Chesapeake Bay and flowing into the sea. The streams on the western side run into the Shenandoah River and then run northward into the Potomac River. West of the Blue Ridge lie the gently rolling hills and valleys of the Great Valley, about 15 to 25 miles wide, from New York south to Alabama. The Valley and Ridge zone lies west of the Great Valley with ridges as high as 3,000 feet and valleys in between. Finally, the western boundary of the Appalachian Mountains is at the Allegheny Plateau, which abuts the Valley and Ridge zone. Moving westward, the Allegheny Plateau rises to 3,000 feet and then slopes gradually into the flatter areas of midwestern America. This plateau forms the continent's eastern drainage divide with rivers on the west side reaching the Gulf of Mexico via the Ohio and Mississippi Rivers, while waters from the east side run into the Atlantic Ocean via Chesapeake Bay.

Scientists believe that humans have passed through these Southern Appalachians for some 10,000 years. The Cherokee probably crossed into these mountains and surrounding lands almost 1,000 years ago. The mountains and valleys became their homelands, ultimately covering what is now seven states with an estimated population of more than 20,000. The first Europeans to see these lands did not arrive until the mid-sixteenth century with Hernando De Soto. However, it wasn't until more than 200 years later that Europeans entered the area to explore more carefully, establish trading posts, and describe the flora and fauna.

Veterans of the Revolutionary War were often paid with land grants, and together with others, the early nineteenth century saw settlers occupying and clearing much of the land, establishing households and farms. Once the forests of the Northeast were depleted, aided by the development of steam-powered machinery and the railroads, lumber operations moved to the southern mountains. By the 1920s, after almost a half century of intensive harvesting, an estimated three-quarters of the southern forests were gone. In spite of this commercial activity, more than 100,000 acres of virgin forest were left untouched, leaving behind some of the last remaining stands of virgin forest in the East. While much of the land was finally set aside and protected, new threats arose in the form of alien plants and insects imported from overseas and declining air quality. With changes induced in these ecosystems, the soil, water, forest cover, resident animals and insects, and the wildflowers are in a continuously changing pattern over time.

With all this, the Southern Appalachians remain one of the gems of North American ecosystems, with lush forests, abundant flora and fauna, and some of the highest mountains in the eastern United States. Sharing the same geological origins, these ancient Southern Appalachians continue to attract hikers and wildflower enthusiasts to witness an incredible variety of plants unmatched anywhere else in North America.

How to Use This Book

This wildflower guide focuses on the plants of the Southern Appalachian Mountains rather than on wildflowers growing in one state or a large, diverse region. The Southern Appalachian Mountains range from the mountains of southwestern Virginia and southern West Virginia south to Georgia and Alabama. They are the home of the greatest variety of wildflowers to be found anywhere in North America.

The entire Appalachian Mountains from Labrador to Georgia and Alabama share many of the same geological origins and contain some of the most splendid ecosystems in the eastern United States. The latitude, the geology, the amount of annual rainfall and other climatic factors, and the drainage of the river systems in these mountains determine which plants grow in each part of the chain.

Starting in early April at the southern end of the chain in Alabama and ending sometime in late June or early July at the northern end, flowering small trees and bushes provide brilliant displays along the roads that wind throughout these mountains. This guide includes many of these bushes, vines, and small trees, as well as those wildflowers that grow in the woods and other habitats of the mountains.

Many plants such as wild azaleas and wild orchids bloom only for a week or two. In the mountains, altitude as well as latitude influence when these plants bloom. Every thousand feet you go up a mountain is equivalent to going 100 miles north. As a result some plants will bloom up to six weeks earlier at low altitudes in Georgia than will the same plant in northern Virginia. In order to help the user of this guide see these limited floral displays, we have included more precise information on when they bloom throughout the Appalachian chain and some specific sites where they can be found. There is also a section in the back of the book that details how to contact these sites to get additional information.

The section of the book that illustrates and describes the plants separates flowers by color. When a flower has more than one color or can be of several different colors, it appears in the section of the dominant color in the illustration, and the text describes any other colors associated with the flowers of this plant. Within the section of a given color, flowers are then sorted alphabetically into groups by their botanical family name and then further ordered alphabetically by genus and species within each family.

The accompanying description gives first the common name of the flower, which is the name or names most frequently used in the region where the plant grows. Usually, a plant has a number of common names. Many of these common names relate to the supposed properties of the plant, others to their habitat or appearance. The botanical name of the flower is given next in italics, with the generic name first, followed by the species. The family is then listed with the common family name followed by the botanical family name in parentheses. The botanical name of each plant is also usually descriptive of the appearance of the plant but uses Greek or Latin terms.

The **Description** provides visual cues essential to identifying the plant: plant height, the shape and placement of leaves, flower size, and the shape and color of petals. Other distinguishing characteristics such as wings (thin flaps at the edge of a leafstalk or along a stem or other part of the plant) and whether the plant is classified as a vine or a bush are also included as necessary. We used as few technical terms in the description as possible. However, there are accepted standard names for the parts of the plant and for some distinguishing characteristics of leaves, flowers, and other plant parts. We have used these terms when it helps distinguish one plant from similar ones. A glossary of standard botanical terms used in this guide is at the end of the book.

If the stem of the entire plant or the stalk of a leaf or a flower provides distinguishing characteristics of the plant, it is described. Plants can have leaves on their stem, at the base of the plant, or both at the base and on the stem. Stem leaves can be opposite each other, alternate on the stem, or grow in a circular arrangement and form what is called a **whorl**. Noticing leaf placement helps distinguish those plants that have flowers that are similar in shape and color but differ in the placement and shape of their leaves. For example dandelions *(Leontodon)* and hawkweeds *(Hieracium)* have similar yellow flowers, but their leaf placement and shape differ enough to allow positive identification.

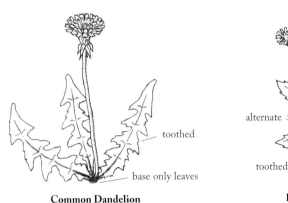

toothed

base only leaves

Common Dandelion

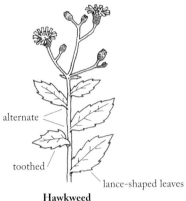

alternate

toothed

lance-shaped leaves

Hawkweed

In describing leaf shape, the term **entire** is used when the outer margin is continuous and unbroken, **toothed** when the leaf has pointed breaks in the margin, and **lobed** when the breaks are rounded. A leaf that is cut one or more times is called **divided** and its parts are called **leaflets.** If it is so finely divided that it resembles a fern, the leaf is described as **fernlike.** Yellow Wood Sorrel *(Oxalis stricta)* and Dwarf Cinquefoil *(Potentilla canadensis)* both have yellow flowers with five petals, but the Sorrel leaves are divided into three rounded leaflets while the Cinquefoil has five toothed leaflets.

Flowers are usually the showiest part of the plant, and the flower descriptions emphasize the shape, number of petals, size, and color. Other descriptive terms for parts of the flower such as the **calyx** and **corolla** are sometimes used. The outer colored part, the **petals,** all together form the **corolla,** and the outer leaflike parts of the flower, called **sepals,** make up the **calyx.** Occasionally the reproductive parts of a flower, the male **stamen** and **pollen** or female **ovary, pistil,** and **stigma,** are mentioned when these parts can be used to distinguish one flower from another. There are also a few plants that have tiny flowers growing on a stalk shaped like a club, called a **spadix,** which is enclosed in a partial hood called a **spathe.**

Most flowers described in the book are symmetrical or have a unique shape, such as when one petal forms a protruding lip, or when a mass of

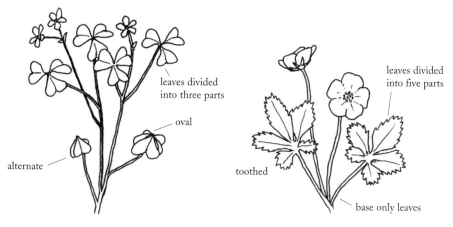

leaves divided
into three parts

oval

alternate

Yellow Wood Sorrel

leaves divided
into five parts

toothed

base only leaves

Dwarf Cinquefoil

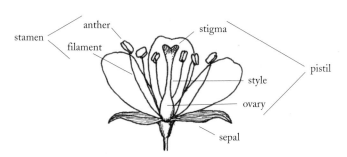

stamen

anther

filament

stigma

style

ovary

pistil

sepal

Reproductive System

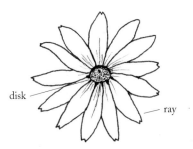

disk

ray

Composite Flower

lip

Lipped Flower

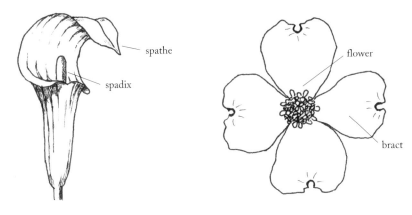

Jack-in-the-Pulpit   **Flowering Dogwood**

flowers forms a head in which the parts of the flower cannot be distinguished one from the other. Flowers can be regular, with **rays, petals,** or **bracts** (which look like petals) arranged in a symmetrical pattern, each similar to all others in shape. A bract can have almost any shape and look like a leaf or petal of a flower. The bracts of a plant are identified in the description only when they can be mistaken for a petal in a regularly shaped flower, as in the Dogwood *(Cornus florida)*, or mistaken for an identifying leaf. In the composite family, the rays, which are flowers, circle the disk, which is the center of the flower head. The daisy is a commonly found example of a composite.

Bloom Season indicates the time of year one is most likely to see the flowers at some location in its range.

The **Habitat/Range** section provides information on the environment (wooded areas, open places, marshes, etc.) in which the plant is generally found and the entire range of locations where it has been seen.

The **Comments** section provides a variety of information, some of which can aid in the identification of plants of the same genus that are not illustrated in this guide. Some plants in the Appalachian Mountains may differ visually from the species illustrated in this guide by something as simple as the shape of the leaf. Many different kinds of violets and goldenrods fall into this category. The comment section lists some of these plants and describes their unique characteristics. For plants that are less common or that bloom for a short period of time and whose bloom season varies from one location to another, specific site locations and bloom times are provided. When a location is listed for these plants, it is not the only spot where the plant may be found, but simply one of many. Whether a plant is commonly used for food and medicine or special information about the common or botanical name of the plant is also noted in the coments section.

Good Wildflower Hunting Sites and Times

At the back of the book, the "Places Cited" section lists the locations of the various places appearing under **Comments** where we have seen these flowers. We also list addresses, phone numbers, and Web sites for these areas. These contacts are the best way to find out about road and weather conditions and particularly about which wildflowers are in bloom. The e-mail addresses for the federal and state agencies responsible for management of the parks and forests in the Central Appalachian region are also provided.

We also include a list of additional reading for those wishing to delve deeper into the subject.

WHITE FLOWERS

Snow Drop Tree

Water Willow

WATER WILLOW
Justicia americana
Acanthus Family (Acanthaceae)

Description: The narrow, lanceolate leaves are opposite each other on the stem of this 1–3' plant. The ½–¾" white flowers have purple spots and 1 of the 4 petals forms a lip.

Bloom Season: July–August

Habitat/Range: A plant of wet places growing from Quebec to Michigan and south to Texas and Georgia.

Comments: Water Willow is often found in the water or along the gravelly or sandy banks of rivers or streams that flood. It grows in water and on moist banks and at the edges of streams at low elevations in Great Smoky Mountains National Park. The beautiful flower can be best appreciated when viewed through a magnifying glass.

BROAD-LEAVED ARROWHEAD OR COMMON ARROWHEAD
Sagittaria latifolia
Water Plantain Family (Alismataceae)

Description: The arrow-shaped leaves at the base of this 8–18" water plant can be broad or narrow. The 1–2" flowers have 3 white petals.

Bloom Season: July-September

Habitat/Range: Arrowheads grow at the edges of streams, rivers, and ponds. Common Arrowhead is found throughout North America and as far south as Mexico.

Comments: This plant is also known as Duck Potato because of the white starchy part of the root of the plant. These "potatoes" were eaten and relished by numerous Native Americans from the Pacific Coast to the Atlantic Coast.

Broad-Leaved Arrowhead or Common Arrowhead

SPIKENARD
Aralia racemosa
Ginseng Family (Araliaceae)

Description: The leaves of this 3–6' plant are divided into large toothed and heart-shaped leaflets that alternate on the stem. The 1", 5-petal flowers are greenish white and form small round clusters. There are usually 2 or 3 clusters on each flower stalk. The flower stalks form a long cluster at the end of the stem.

Bloom Season: June–August

Habitat/Range: In rich woods from New Brunswick to Georgia.

Comments: Spikenards are found in Great Smoky Mountains National Park. Native Americans used this plant—known for its aromatic root—as a root tea for a number of ailments and also used it to improve the flavor of other medicines.

Spikenard

Dwarf Ginseng

DWARF GINSENG
Panax trifolium
Ginseng Family (Araliaceae)

Description: The leaves of this 6–8" plant are toothed and divided in 3 sections and form a whorl of 3 on the stem. The tiny flowers have 5 white petals, and together they form a ball.

Bloom Season: April–May

Habitat/Range: In moist woods from Nova Scotia to Georgia.

Comments: Native Americans made a tea from this plant and chewed the roots to treat headaches and fainting. However, popular ginseng products sold on the market are not made from Dwarf Ginseng. This plant's medicinal uses have not been studied by modern medicine.

Poke Milkweed

POKE MILKWEED
Asclepias exaltata
Milkweed Family (Asclepiadaceae)

Description: The entire, elliptical, tapered leaves are opposite each other on the stem of this 3–5' plant. The ¾" drooping flowers are greenish white, and each of the 5 petals has a pointed crown and a dangling point.

Bloom Season: June–July

Habitat/Range: In dry woods from Maine to Minnesota and south to Georgia and Arkansas.

Comments: Found at both medium and high locations in Great Smoky Mountains National Park and in the woods around Peaks of Otter on the Blue Ridge Parkway in Virginia.

WHITE MILKWEED
Asclepias variegata
Milkweed Family (Asclepiadaceae)

Description: The oblong leaves are opposite each other on the stem of this 1–3' field plant. The ½–¾" flowers are white with a purple-tinged center. Each flower has 5 petals, and each petal has a pointed crown and a dangling point. The flowers are arranged in a round cluster.

Bloom Season: May–July

Habitat/Range: In dry woods from Connecticut to Illinois and south to Florida and Texas.

Comments: This milkweed can be distinguished from the other white-flowered milkweed, Poke Milkweed, because the flower cluster is erect and there are more flowers in each cluster.

White Milkweed

Mayapple or Mandrake

MAYAPPLE OR MANDRAKE
Podophyllum peltatum
Barberry Family (Berberidaceae)

Description: The large, toothed leaves are opposite each other on the stem of this 1–1½' plant. The 1½–2" flowers have 6–9 waxy, white petals and grow on the stem of the plant, just below the long stalks of the 2 leaves.

Bloom Season: April–June

Habitat/Range: In woods from western Quebec to southern Ontario and south to Florida and Texas.

Comments: The plant comes out of the ground in early spring looking like a closed umbrella. The umbrella opens up into a plant with 1 or 2 large leaves. The flowers, and hence the fruit, are found only on plants that have 2 leaves. The fruit is edible when ripe, but the unripe fruit can cause severe digestive problems. The root of the plant is poisonous.

Smooth Rock Cress

SMOOTH ROCK CRESS
Arabis laevigata
Mustard Family (Brassicaceae)

Description: The lanceolate, toothed leaves are opposite each other and clasp the stem of this 1–3" plant. The ⅛" flowers have 4 greenish white petals and are shaped like small bells with an extended clapper.

Bloom Season: April–June

Habitat/Range: In rocky woods from Quebec to Ontario and south to Georgia and Arkansas.

Comments: This delicate plant often grows at the base of trees and can be easily overlooked. It is one of the very early spring bloomers and sometimes can be found in late March in the Southern Appalachian Mountains.

PENNSYLVANIA BITTERCRESS
Cardamine pensylvanica
Mustard Family (Brassicaceae)

Description: The leaves of this 6–18" plant are divided into 5–15 leaflets that alternate on the stem. The ⅛", 4-petal flowers are white.

Bloom Season: April–June

Habitat/Range: In moist places from Newfoundland to Minnesota and south to Florida.

Comments: This is one of the earliest plants to bloom in the spring, and in many places it is one of the first plants that invades suburban lawns.

Pennsylvania Bittercress

WHITLOW GRASS
Draba verna
Mustard Family (Brassicaceae)

Description: The ovate leaves are at the base of this 3–8" plant. The ⅛" flowers have 4 cleft, white petals.

Bloom Season: April–May

Habitat/Range: Fields and open places from Massachusetts and Vermont to Iowa and south to Georgia, Tennessee, and Missouri.

Comments: This Old World species that is now naturalized in many places in the United States is one of the earliest plants to bloom in the spring. The word *verna* means "spring." At one time a sore under the fingernail or toenail was called a whitlow, the cure for which was the application of *Draba verna*.

Whitlow Grass

Common Elder

COMMON ELDER
Sambucus canadensis
Honeysuckle Family (Caprifoliaceae)

Description: The shiny leaves on this 4–7' shrub or small tree are divided into 5–10 paired leaflets. The leaflets are each elliptical or lanceolate and toothed. The ¼", 5-petal, white flowers form a flat cluster.

Bloom Season: June–July

Habitat/Range: In moist soils from Nova Scotia to Florida and west to Manitoba and Texas.

Comments: The fruit of this shrub is used to make elderberry wine, the drink made infamous in the movie and play *Arsenic and Old Lace*.

Red-Berried Elder

RED-BERRIED ELDER
Sambucus pubens
Honeysuckle Family (Caprifoliaceae)

Description: The leaves on this 3–10' shrub are divided into toothed, ovate leaflets. The ¼" flowers have 5 white petals each and form a pyramid cluster.

Bloom Season: May

Habitat/Range: In rocky places from Newfoundland to northern New England; also found in the Great Smoky Mountains.

Comments: This is an example of one of the many plants normally found only in northern locations that can be found at the higher elevations in Great Smoky Mountains National Park. Unlike its cousin Common Elder, whose berries are used to make jam, the berries of this plant are poisonous.

Black Haw

BLACK HAW
Viburnum prunifolium
Honeysuckle Family (Caprifoliaceae)

Description: The leaves on this 6–12' shrub are lanceolate and toothed. The bark is red. The ⅓" flowers have 5 white petals and form an umbel.

Bloom Season: April

Habitat/Range: Upland woods and thickets from Connecticut to Michigan, Iowa, and Kansas, and south to northern Florida and Texas.

Comments: Teas made from the stem, bark, and roots of this plant were used medicinally first by Native Americans and then adopted by European settlers to relieve painful menses and to relieve spasms after childbirth. Modern research confirms its uterine anti-spasmodic properties, but the berries may produce gastric discomfort. These small trees or bushes are found along the Blue Ridge Parkway.

Bladder Campion

BLADDER CAMPION
Silene cucubalus
Pink Family (Caryophyllaceae)

Description: The lanceolate leaves are opposite each other on the stem of this 1–2' plant. The leaves are smooth. The 1–1½" flowers are made up of an inflated bladder with light red lines topped by 5 notched white petals.

Bloom Season: May–June

Habitat/Range: Found on roadsides and open spaces from Newfoundland to British Columbia, south to Virginia, Tennessee, and Kansas, and west to Colorado and Oregon.

Comments: A native of Europe that is now a familiar flower in the United States, Bladder Campion is found along the James River where it flows under the Blue Ridge Parkway in Virginia.

Starry Campion

STARRY CAMPION
Silene stellata
Pink Family (Caryophyllaceae)

Description: The long, ovate leaves form a whorl of 4 on the stem of this 1–3' plant. The 1–1½" flowers have 5 white, fringed petals that form a bell.

Bloom Season: July–September

Habitat/Range: In woods, thickets, and at the edge of roads from Massachusetts to North Dakota and south to Georgia and Oklahoma.

Comments: Starry Campions are found near the Humpback Rock Visitors Center and at other roadside locations along the edge of the Blue Ridge Parkway and along River Road in Great Smoky Mountains National Park.

Star Chickweed or Great Chickweed

STAR CHICKWEED OR GREAT CHICKWEED
Stellaria pubera
Pink Family (Caryophyllaceae)

Description: The long, ovate leaves are opposite each other on the stem of this 6–12" plant. The ½" flowers have bright red stamens and 5 deeply notched, white petals that form a star.

Bloom Season: March–June

Habitat/Range: A plant found in wooded areas and on rocky slopes from New York to Illinois and south to Alabama and Florida.

Comments: This beautiful plant grows in many locations in the Southern Appalachian Mountains. Star Chickweed can be found in April at Hungry Mother State Park and the Cascade Recreation Area of Jefferson National Forest in Virginia, on the nature trail at Fort Mountain State Park, and in the Sosebee Cove area of the Chattahoochee National Forest in Georgia.

YARROW OR MILFOIL
Achillea millefolium
Composite Family (Compositae)

Description: The finely divided leaves alternate on the stem of this 1–3' plant. The small flowers are white or pink and form a flat umbel.

Bloom Season: June–September

Habitat/Range: This plant grows throughout the Northern Hemisphere; it may have originated in Europe.

Comments: Yarrow was reportedly used medicinally in ancient Greece and as recently as in the Civil War to stanch battle wounds.

Yarrow or Milfoil

SOLITARY PUSSYTOES
Antennaria solitaria
Composite Family (Compositae)

Description: The pointed, ovate leaves are at the base of this 4–16" plant. The 1" white flowers form a single tuft.

Bloom Season: April–May

Habitat/Range: In rich wooded areas from Maryland west to Pennsylvania and Indiana, and south to Georgia, Alabama, and Louisiana.

Comments: Like its relative, Field Pussytoes *(Antennaria neglecta),* which also grows in the Southern Appalachian Mountains and whose flowers are made up of several tufts, the plant was boiled in milk and was a folk remedy for diarrhea and dysentery. Native Americans and colonists used a poultice of the leaves to treat bruises, sores, boils, and snakebite.

Solitary Pussytoes

Lowrie's Aster

LOWRIE'S ASTER
Aster lowrieanus
Composite Family (Compositae)

Description: The ovate, toothed, and pointed leaves are attached by a winged stalk and alternate on the stem of this 12–18" plant. The ½–1" flowers have many white or light blue petals around a central disk.

Bloom Season: July–September

Habitat/Range: In open woodlands in Connecticut and south to Georgia and Tennessee.

Comments: As a group, the asters are easy to identify, but the great number of varieties within the genus makes it difficult for the amateur naturalist to identify many of the species. Lowrie's Aster is one of the exceptions, as the ovate leaves have a sharp point and a distinct wing along their stalk.

Large-Leaved Aster or Big-Leaf Aster

LARGE-LEAVED ASTER OR BIG-LEAF ASTER
Aster macrophyllus
Composite Family (Compositae)

Description: The lower, heart-shaped leaf of this aster can be as large as 8" across. The leaves alternate on the stem of this 1–5' plant. The 1" flowers are lavender or white. Each flower has 10–12 petals.

Bloom Season: August–October

Habitat/Range: Found in woods or clearings in New England and Canada and in the Great Smoky Mountains of Tennessee and North Carolina.

Comments: Asters hybridize, making positive identification difficult even for trained botanists. The lower, large, heart-shaped leaf of this white aster is unique and makes a positive identification easy.

PALE INDIAN PLANTAIN
Cacalia atriplicifolia
Composite Family (Compositae)

Description: The lobed leaves alternate on the stem of this 3–6' tall plant. The ½" white flowers form a flat cluster.

Bloom Season: July

Habitat/Range: In woods from New York south to Florida.

Comments: The leaves of the plant were used by Native Americans as a poultice for cuts and bruises and to draw out blood or poisonous substances. In July it can be found blooming along the edges of Route 411 in Tennessee and in the Green Briar Picnic Area of Great Smoky Mountains National Park.

Pale Indian Plantain

Daisy or Ox-Eye Daisy

DAISY OR OX-EYE DAISY
Chrysanthemum leucanthemum
Composite Family (Compositae)

Description: The toothed, lobed leaves alternate on the stem of this 1–2' plant. The 2–3" flowers have white petals and a yellow disk. Each flower has 15–30 petals.

Bloom Season: May–September

Habitat/Range: In open places throughout the area, but less common in the south. It was naturalized from Europe and also grows in Asia.

Comments: Having a home wildflower garden is gaining in popularity and the Daisy, while not sweet smelling, makes a wonderful addition. It has a very long blooming season and is a long-lasting cut flower. Very few other wildflowers that grow in the Appalachian Mountains have either of these characteristics.

Daisy Fleabane or Sweet Scabious

DAISY FLEABANE OR SWEET SCABIOUS
Erigeron annuus
Composite Family (Compositae)

Description: The lanceolate leaves alternate on the stem of this 1–4' plant and have a few teeth on their margins . The ½–¾" flowers are made up of 50–100 white or pink petals surrounding a yellow disk.

Bloom Season: May–August

Habitat/Range: In meadows and open woods from Nova Scotia to British Columbia and south to Florida, Texas, and California. Naturalized in Europe.

Comments: Often mistaken for asters, which normally bloom in late summer and fall, Daisy Fleabane is a plant of late spring and summer. Other than in the most arid desert, Daisy Fleabane is the native plant most likely to be found in parks and wild places anywhere from southern Canada to the southern United States.

HYSSOP-LEAVED BONESET OR HYSSOP-LEAVED THOROUGHWORT
Eupatorium hyssopifolium
Composite Family (Compositae)

Description: The grasslike leaves form whorls of 3 or 4 on the stem of this 2–3' plant. The 2–3" flowers are white and form a flat-topped umbel with about 5 flowers in each head.

Bloom Season: August–October

Habitat/Range: In dry fields from Massachusetts to Florida and Texas.

Comments: North of the Southern Appalachian Mountains, Hyssop-Leaved Boneset is found mostly in the Piedmont or on the Coastal Plain rather than in the Appalachian Mountains.

Hyssop-Leaved Boneset or
Hyssop-Leaved Thoroughwort

White Boneset or Common Boneset

WHITE BONESET OR COMMON BONESET
Eupatorium perfoliatum
Composite Family (Compositae)

Description: The lanceolate, toothed leaves unite around the stem of this 1–3' plant. The ¼" white flowers form a flat cluster.

Bloom Season: July–September

Habitat/Range: In wet places from New Brunswick, Nova Scotia, and Manitoba to Florida and Nebraska. Also found in Texas.

Comments: The plant is native to North America. Boneset was a plant commonly used in folk medicine, especially for treating a disease called "break-bone fever."

Round-Leaved Boneset or Round-Leaved Snakeroot

ROUND-LEAVED BONESET OR ROUND-LEAVED SNAKEROOT
Eupatorium rotundifolium
Composite Family (Compositae)

Description: The stemless, toothed, ovate leaves are opposite each other on the stem of this 1–2' plant. The ¼" flowers are white and form clusters of 5–7 flowers.

Bloom Season: September

Habitat/Range: In dry soils from Rhode Island to Pennsylvania and in the Southern Appalachian Mountains and Florida.

Comments: North of the Southern Appalachian Mountains, Round-Leaved Boneset is found mostly in the Piedmont or on the Coastal Plain rather than in the Appalachian Mountains.

LATE-FLOWERING BONESET
Eupatorium serotinum
Composite Family (Compositae)

Description: The stalked, lanceolate, toothed leaves are opposite each other on the stem of this 1–3' plant. The tiny flowers are white and form a flat umbel.

Bloom Season: September–October

Habitat/Range: In meadows and abandoned fields from Massachusetts to Wisconsin and south to Florida, Texas, and Mexico.

Comments: True to its name, this is a fall-flowering boneset. A similar boneset with leaves on long stalks, White Snakeroot *(Eupatorium rugosum)*, starts blooming in July in the Southern Appalachian Mountains.

Late-Flowering Boneset

SWEET EVERLASTING OR CATFOOT

Gnaphalium obtusifolium
Composite Family (Compositae)

Description: The lanceolate, long, and narrow leaves alternate on the stem of this 1–2' plant. The ½–¾" white flowers form several small clusters at the top of the stem.

Bloom Season: August–October

Habitat/Range: In dry, mostly open places from Nova Scotia to Florida.

Comments: Sweet Everlasting is rare in the north and more common in the Southern Appalachian Mountains, while Pearly Everlasting *(Anaphalis margaritacea)*, a similar plant, is rare in the South and is common from Pennsylvania north in the Appalachian Mountains. Sweet Everlasting grows at low and middle elevations in Great Smoky Mountains National Park and along the Blue Ridge Parkway in North Carolina around mile 200.

Sweet Everlasting or Catfoot

Wild Quinine or American Feverfew

WILD QUININE OR AMERICAN FEVERFEW

Parthenium integrifolium
Composite Family (Compositae)

Description: The lanceolate, slightly toothed leaves alternate on the stem of this 1–5' plant. The leaves are rough and the lowest leaves have long stalks. The flowers have 5 white, tiny petals and form an umbel.

Bloom Season: June–September

Habitat/Range: In dry woodlands and prairies from New York to Minnesota and south to Georgia and Texas.

Comments: Wild Quinine grows at low altitudes in Great Smoky Mountains National Park. It particularly seems to like the growing conditions around the rock outcrops on ridges. Native Americans and the early settlers used Wild Quinine medicinally. It is sometimes found in today's echinacea compounds.

Silverrod or White Goldenrod

SILVERROD OR WHITE GOLDENROD
Solidago bicolor
Composite Family (Compositae)

Description: The toothed leaves alternate on the stem of this 2–4' plant. The 1/2" white flowers form long cylindrical clusters.

Bloom Season: August–September

Habitat/Range: In dry soils from Prince Edward Island to Georgia and west to Tennessee.

Comments: Silverrod is a very common plant along the entire range of the Appalachian Mountains. A few of the many locations where it can be seen are: Vermont's Groton State Forest in the northern part of the range, New York's Catskills Mountains and Bear Mountain State Park in the Central Appalachians, and in the South along the Blue Ridge Parkway in Virginia and North Carolina.

HEDGE BINDWEED OR LADY'S NIGHTCAP
Convolvulus sepium
Morning Glory Family (Convolvulaceae)

Description: This trailing vine has alternate, lobed, arrow-shaped leaves. The bottom lobes of the leaf have blunt edges. The 1–2" white flowers have 5 petals and are trumpet shaped.

Bloom Season: July–September

Habitat/Range: In fields and thickets from Maine to North Carolina. The plant is also found in British Columbia, Illinois, Nebraska, and New Mexico.

Comments: The shape of the flower is the reason for the common name used in many southern communities, Lady's Nightcap.

Hedge Bindweed or Lady's Nightcap

COMMON DODDER OR LOVE VINE

Cuscuta gronovii
Morning Glory Family (Convolvulaceae)

Common Dodder or Love Vine

Description: There are no leaves on this orange-colored vine. The 1/16–1/8", bell-shaped flowers are white. Each flower has 5 tiny petals.

Bloom Season: September–October

Habitat/Range: In open areas and along roadsides from Nova Scotia to Montana and south to Florida and Texas.

Comments: A parasitic vine that gets its nourishment through little suckers plunged into the plants it entwines, this plant can be found along the Blue Ridge Parkway, often completely wrapping up the bush or plant it has captured.

Small White Morning Glory

SMALL WHITE MORNING GLORY

Ipomoea lacunosa
Morning Glory Family (Convolvulaceae)

Description: The heart-shaped, lobed leaves are attached singly on the stem of this vine. The 1/2–1" flowers have 5 white petals and are trumpet shaped.

Bloom Season: August–October

Habitat/Range: In moist areas, especially in thickets and in fields from New Jersey west to Kansas and south to Florida and Texas.

Comments: Many species of this plant are hybridized and cultivated as ornamental plants, and the most popular varieties appearing in gardens in the northern United States are descended from a Mexican species. *I. lacunosa* is found at low altitudes in Great Smoky Mountains National Park. The genus *Ipomoea* also includes the sweet potato.

Alternate-Leaf Dogwood

ALTERNATE-LEAF DOGWOOD
Cornus alternifolia
Dogwood Family (Cornaceae)

Description: The leaves on this 4–8' shrub are ovate. The ¼" flowers have 4 white petals and form an umbel.

Bloom Season: July

Habitat/Range: Along moist woods and stream banks from Newfoundland to southern Ontario and Minnesota and south to Alabama, Arkansas, and Florida.

Comments: Alternate-Leaf Dogwood is also known as Blue Dogwood, possibly because the fruits are blue-black. It grows in Great Smoky Mountains National Park and in the Mount Rogers Recreation Area of Jefferson National Forest in Virginia.

WHITE DOGWOOD
Cornus florida
Dogwood Family (Cornaceae)

Description: The entire, ovate leaves are opposite each other on the stem of this 6–20' small tree. What looks like a 2–4", 4-petal, white or pink flower is really made up of white or pink notched bracts. The actual flowers are tiny and can be found in the center of the blossom.

Bloom Season: April–May

Habitat/Range: In wooded areas and along roads from Maine and Ontario to Florida.

Comments: White Dogwood is a very common tree in the Appalachian Mountains from southern Pennsylvania to Georgia and Alabama. North of southern Pennsylvania, it needs a very sheltered spot to survive the winters. In early April, look for blooming White Dogwoods in Fort Mountain State Park, Georgia, and at low and middle altitudes in Great Smoky Mountains National Park.

White Dogwood

Wild Stonecrop

WILD STONECROP
Sedum ternatum
Orpine Family (Crassulaceae)

Description: The ovate, fleshy leaves are opposite each other on the stem of this creeping plant. The ½" star-shaped flowers have 4 or 5 white or pink petals.

Bloom Season: April–June

Habitat/Range: On banks and rocky hills, from New York to Michigan south to Georgia and Tennessee.

Comments: In the spring Wild Stonecrop is frequently seen among the rocks that border the Appalachian Trail from Massachusetts south to Georgia. Also look for this plant in Fort Desoto State Park in Alabama and in the Cascade Recreation Area of Jefferson National Forest in Virginia. The leaves of the Wild Stonecrop that grows along the trails in forests tend to be less fleshy than those on plants that grow on ledges in sunny areas, and some botanists consider these 2 varieties separate species.

Oconee Bells

OCONEE BELLS
Shortia galacifolia
Diapensia Family (Diapensiaceae)

Description: The heart-shaped, toothed, glossy, evergreen leaves are at the base of this 6–10" plant. The 1–1½" flowers have 5 white petals that form a fringed bell.

Bloom Season: April–May

Habitat/Range: Along stream banks in rich woods in very few counties in the mountains of North Carolina and Georgia.

Comments: This plant was once found in woods in many places east of the Mississippi River. Like many beautiful wild plants dug up for transplanting in gardens, Oconee Bells has disappeared from all but the most secluded forests. Some nature centers and the National Arboretum in Washington, D.C., grow Oconee Bells so that they can be seen by more than backwoods hikers.

TRAILING ARBUTUS OR MAYFLOWER
Epigaea repens
Heath Family (Ericaceae)

Description: The ovate, leathery leaves alternate on the stem of this creeping evergreen plant. The ½" flowers are white and bell shaped. Each flower has 5 petals.

Bloom Season: March–May

Habitat/Range: In sandy or rocky wooded areas. Once a common plant widely spread from Saskatchewan to Newfoundland and south to Kentucky and Florida, it now grows only in northern areas away from population centers. In some states it is against the law to pick or damage this plant.

Comments: Trailing Arbutus is found in mid-April along the low banks lining some of the trails in the Beartree Recreation Area of Jefferson National Forest in Virginia and along the banks lining the Roaring Forks Motor Nature Trail in Great Smoky National Park in Tennessee.

Trailing Arbutus or Mayflower

Wintergreen or Teaberry

WINTERGREEN OR TEABERRY
Gaultheria procumbens
Heath Family (Ericaceae)

Description: The slightly toothed, shiny, ovate leaves form a whorl of 3 on the stem of this 2–6" creeping plant. The ½" white flowers form a bell with a waxy appearance.

Bloom Season: July–August

Habitat/Range: In wooded areas, especially under evergreen trees, from Nova Scotia south to Georgia.

Comments: Native Americans and early settlers used the oil extracted from this plant to flavor foods with wintergreen. Today commercial wintergreen used in gum and for flavoring is synthesized.

Mountain Laurel

MOUNTAIN LAUREL
Kalmia latifolia
Heath Family (Ericaceae)

Description: The leaves on this 3–15' shrub are evergreen and shiny. The ¾", white, cup-like flowers have 5 white (at times pink tinted) petals that form a terminal cluster.

Bloom Season: April–June

Habitat/Range: In wooded areas, preferring rocky or sandy soils, from New Brunswick to Ontario and south to Florida and Louisiana.

Comments: This beautiful but poisonous shrub can be found throughout the Appalachian Mountains. It blooms in late April in Georgia and Alabama and around the first week of June in northern Pennsylvania and New York. The woody branches should not be used for cooking food. Children can be poisoned by eating the leaves.

FETTERBUSH OR DOWNY LEUCOTHOE

Leucothoe axillaris
Heath Family (Ericaceae)

Description: The toothed, lanceolate leaves alternate on the stem of this 2–5' shrub. The shrub loses its leaves in the fall. The ½", urn-shaped flowers have 5 white petals.

Bloom Season: April–May

Habitat/Range: In moist woods from Virginia to Florida.

Comments: Fetterbush grows along streams and under wet rock overhangs. It can be found blooming in mid-April under the rock overhangs along River Road in Great Smoky Mountains National Park. Another shrub, called Fetterbush or Dog-Hobble *(Leucothoe recurva)*, has evergreen leaves and similarly shaped flowers and also grows from the cliffs that line the roads in Great Smoky Mountains National Park and can be found along the Roaring Fork Motor Nature Trail in May.

Fetterbush or Downy Leucothoe

Giant Rhododendron or Rosebay

GIANT RHODODENDRON OR ROSEBAY

Rhododendron maximum
Heath Family (Ericaceae)

Description: This 5–40' shrub has shiny, dark green, lanceolate leaves. The 1½–2" flowers have 5 white or pink petals and form a cluster.

Bloom Season: Late May–August

Habitat/Range: In wooded areas and along streams from Nova Scotia to Ontario and south to Georgia and Alabama.

Comments: There are often traffic jams at Great Smoky Mountains National Park when the rhododendron and summer azaleas bloom in late May and early June. For alternate places to see these wonderful displays, see the parks and forests listed for Georgia and Alabama in the back of this book.

HIGHBUSH BLUEBERRY OR SWAMP BLUEBERRY
Vaccinium corymbosum
Heath Family (Ericaceae)

Description: The leaves on this 3-15' shrub are ovate. The ½" flowers have 5 white or pink petals that form a narrow bell.

Bloom Season: April–May

Habitat/Range: In swamps, thickets, and wooded areas from Maine south to Louisiana.

Comments: A great deal of the commercially grown blueberries sold in the East are the offspring of 4 plants cultivated from the Highbush Blueberry bushes that grow abundantly in the Pine Barrens of New Jersey. Blueberry bushes are common in the Appalachian Mountains. Look for the flowers on this shrub in early April and the fruits in June in Fort Mountain State Park in Georgia.

Highbush Blueberry or Swamp Blueberry

COMMON PIPEWORT
Eriocaulon septangulare
Pipewort Family (Eriocaulaceae)

Description: The grasslike leaves are at the base of this 6–10" plant. The flowers are whitish, about 1¼" high, and form a button at the top of the stem of the plant.

Bloom Season: June–September

Habitat/Range: In still water or on banks from Newfoundland to Minnesota and south to Florida and Texas.

Comments: Pipeworts like standing water and grow in wet places in the Chattahoochee National Forest in Georgia.

Common Pipewort

FLOWERING SPURGE
Euphorbia corollata
Spurge Family (Euphorbiaceae)

Description: The entire leaves on the stem under the flowers form a whorl of 3. Below these leaves, where the stem branches, the leaves alternate on this 1–3' plant. The ¼–½" flowers have 5 white bracts that look like petals. These bracts surround a cluster of tiny flowers.

Bloom Season: July–October

Habitat/Range: Dry fields and open, wooded areas from New York to Minnesota and south to Florida and Texas.

Comments: This plant is a relative of Poinsettia *(Euphorbia pulcherrima),* a popular houseplant at Christmastime. The flowers on the Poinsettia are in the center, small and similar to those on Flowering Spurge. The large, bright red bracts of the Poinsettia make it look very different from its much smaller relative with small white bracts. Flowering Spurge commonly grows in open areas along the Blue Ridge Parkway.

Flowering Spurge

BUSH CLOVER
Lespedeza cuneata
Pea Family (Fabaceae)

Description: The leaves, which alternate on the stem of this 1–4' plant, are divided into 3 rounded leaflets. The ½", pea-shaped flowers are white with purple markings.

Bloom Season: September

Habitat/Range: In open places, mostly in the southeast United States and Asia.

Comments: Sometimes called Chinese Bush Clover, this plant was imported from Asia, escaped from cultivation, and now grows at low elevations in the Smoky Mountains and on the Piedmont and Coastal Plains as far north as Maryland.

Bush Clover

Fringed Phacelia

FRINGED PHACELIA
Phacelia fimbriata
Waterleaf Family (Hydrophyllaceae)

Description: The lobed leaves are opposite on the stem of this 6–8" plant. The 1½" flowers have 5 white petals that form a flared, fringed cup.

Bloom Season: April–May

Habitat/Range: In the woods of the Appalachian Mountains from southwestern Virginia to Georgia and Alabama.

Comments: This beautiful plant is commonly found only in the geographic area covered by this book. At Chimney Top Picnic Area on the Tennessee side of Great Smoky National Park in mid-April, one of the hillsides is covered with blooming Fringed Phacelia.

HORSEMINT
Monarda punctata
Mint Family (Labiatae)

Description: The lanceolate, toothed leaves are opposite each other on the stem of this 1–3' plant. The ¾–1" white flowers grow in a whorl and have pointed petals spotted with purple. The bracts are whitish or lilac and very conspicuous.

Bloom Season: August–September

Habitat/Range: In dry fields and roadsides from western Vermont to Minnesota and south to Florida, Texas, and Arizona.

Comments: Named for the Spanish botanist Nicolas Monardes, who authored the first book on medicinal plants from the New World in the mid-16th century. Native Americans made a leaf tea from Horsemint to relieve colds and fevers. This plant grows at low altitudes in the Great Smoky Mountains National Park.

Horsemint

Narrow-Leaved Mountain Mint

NARROW-LEAVED MOUNTAIN MINT
Pycnanthemum tenuifolium
Mint Family (Labiatae)

Description: The very narrow leaves are opposite each other on the stem of this 1–3' plant. The tiny flowers are white and form a small head.

Bloom Season: July–September

Habitat/Range: Found in dry, wooded areas from New Hampshire west to Illinois and south to Florida and Alabama.

Comments: The common name reference to "mountain" is not accurate since many of the *Pycnanthemum* are found in lowlands. The plant grows along the Blue Ridge Parkway in Virginia just north of the Peaks of Otter Lodge and many other places along the Blue Ridge Parkway and in Great Smoky Mountains National Park. Another white-flowered mountain mint, Short-Toothed Mountain Mint *(Pycnanthemum muticum)*, also blooms along the Blue Ridge. Its leaves have very slight teeth.

Fly Poison

FLY POISON
Amianthium muscaetoxicum
Lily Family (Lilliaceae)

Description: The wide, grasslike leaves are at the base of this 1½–4' plant. The 1" flowers have 6 white petals that turn green as the flowers age. The flowers form a terminal spike.

Bloom Season: June–July

Habitat/Range: In open wooded areas and meadows from southern New York to Missouri and south to Florida, Mississippi, and Arkansas.

Comments: All parts of this plant are poisonous, but the bulbs are especially so, containing poisonous alkaloids that have been known to cause cardiac irregularities in humans.

WILD LILY-OF-THE-VALLEY OR CANADA MAYFLOWER
Maianthemum canadense
Lily Family (Lilliaceae)

Description: The entire, heart-shaped leaves alternate on the stem of this 3–6" plant. The base leaf clasps the stem. The ¹⁄₁₆" white flowers form a small upright cluster.

Bloom Season: April–June

Habitat/Range: In moist wooded areas and thickets from Newfoundland to the Northwest Territory and south to North Carolina, Tennessee, Iowa, and South Dakota.

Comments: This small plant often grows in large groups on the woodland floor, spreading a carpet of white blooms. It starts to bloom in late April in the Southern Appalachian Mountains, in late May in the Central Appalachian Mountains, and in late June in the Northern Appalachian Mountains.

Wild Lily-of-the-Valley or Canada Mayflower

Star-of-Bethlehem

STAR-OF-BETHLEHEM
Ornithogalum umbellatum
Lily Family (Lilliaceae)

Description: The grasslike leaves are at the base of this 4–12" plant. The 1¼–1½" flowers have 6 white petals that form a star with 6 stamens in the center.

Bloom Season: May–June

Habitat/Range: On the Coastal Plain and in the Piedmont from New Hampshire to Virginia. Also at low altitudes in the Great Smoky Mountains.

Comments: This plant is a native of Europe and has been naturalized in the eastern United States, where it grows in abundance.

False Solomon's Seal

FALSE SOLOMON'S SEAL
Smilacina racemosa
Lily Family (Lilliaceae)

Description: The entire, ovate leaves alternate on the stem of this 1–1½' plant. The tiny flowers have 6 white petals and form a branched terminal cluster.

Bloom Season: April–June

Habitat/Range: In moist woods and thickets from Nova Scotia to British Columbia and south to Georgia, Missouri, and Arizona.

Comments: False Solomon's Seal blooms in late April in Georgia and Alabama. Traveling north through the Appalachian Mountains, it blooms late in May in northern Pennsylvania and in June in Maine.

FEATHERFLEECE
Stenanthium gramineum
Lily Family (Lilliaceae)

Description: The grasslike leaves alternate on the stem of this 2–6' plant. The tiny white or green flowers form a narrow 6-petal bell. The placement of the racemes of flowers gives the plant the appearance of a large feather.

Bloom Season: June–September

Habitat/Range: In moist forests and thickets ranging from Pennsylvania to Missouri and south to Texas and Florida.

Comments: Also called Featherbells. In late August and early September, a field covered with many splendid examples of Featherfleece can be seen around mile 200 of the Blue Ridge Parkway in North Carolina.

Featherfleece

Wake Robin or Red Trillium

WAKE ROBIN OR RED TRILLIUM
Trillium erectum
Lily Family (Lilliaceae)

Description: The ovate, almost stalkless leaves form a whorl of 3 on the stem of this 6–18" plant. The 1–1½" flowers have 3 petals that can be red, maroon, or white.

Bloom Season: April–May

Habitat/Range: In wooded areas from Maine to North Carolina.

Comments: In spite of its common alternate name, Red Trillium, the flowers are often white with a prominent black center and 6 yellow stamens. The flowers give off an unpleasant scent if bruised. The red or maroon variety is a very common trillium in the woods of the Central Appalachian Mountains. The white variety is much more common in the Southern Appalachian Mountains.

Large-Flowered Trillium

LARGE-FLOWERED TRILLIUM
Trillium grandiflorum
Lily Family (Lilliaceae)

Description: The ovate leaves form a whorl of 3 on the stem of this 8–18" plant. The 1½–2½" white flowers have 3 petals and are bell shaped. The flowers turn pink as they age.

Bloom Season: April–June

Habitat/Range: In wooded areas from Quebec and Ontario to Minnesota and south to North Carolina and Missouri.

Comments: Large-Flowered Trillium can be found in mid-April along the Roaring Forks Motor Nature Trail and in the Cades Cove area of Great Smoky Mountains National Park, Tennessee, as well as in the Sosebee Cove area of the Chattahoochee National Forest, Georgia.

DWARF TRILLIUM OR SNOW TRILLIUM
Trillium nivale
Lily Family (Lilliaceae)

Description: The 2–3" ovate leaves form a whorl of 3 on the stem of this 2–6" plant. The 2" white flowers have 3 petals.

Bloom Season: April

Habitat/Range: In wooded areas and thickets from Pennsylvania and Ohio to Minnesota and south to Kentucky and Nebraska.

Comments: The plant is also called Early Wake Robin and it does look like a miniature white Wake Robin. It can be found in Jefferson National Forest in southwestern Virginia.

Dwarf Trillium or Snow Trillium

Yucca

YUCCA
Yucca filamentosa
Lily Family (Lilliaceae)

Description: The long, entire, lanceolate leaves are at the base of this 2–6' plant. The leaves have threads on the leaf margin. The 2–3" flowers form white, 4-petal bells. Together, the flowers form a large, showy pyramid cluster.

Bloom Season: June–September

Habitat/Range: In sandy soils from southern Pennsylvania to Florida on the east coast of the United States and in many other locations in the midwestern and western United States.

Comments: Yuccas can be found in the Cades Cove area of Great Smoky Mountains National Park and in the Mount Rogers Recreation Area of Jefferson National Forest, Virginia. Native Americans used the root in salves for skin diseases and sprains.

Fragrant Water Lily

FRAGRANT WATER LILY
Nymphaea odorata
Water Lily Family (Nymphaeaceae)

Description: The leaves are at the base of the plant. The leaf is in the form of a circle with a cleft. The underside of the leaf is red or purple, and the leaves are shiny. The 3–5" flowers have many pink or white petals and a center grouping of yellow stamens.

Bloom Season: June–August

Habitat/Range: In ponds and other quiet waters throughout the United States.

Comments: The flowers are usually white, and the petals seem to slowly melt down to the yellow stamen. A flower opens in the morning and lasts for a few days.

FRINGE TREE
Chionanthus virginicus
Olive Family (Oleaceae)

Description: This 4–10' shrub or small tree has elliptical leaves. The narrow, 2–3" long white flowers hang down in small bunches that blow on the breeze.

Bloom Season: April–May

Habitat/Range: In moist thickets and along streams and rivers from New Jersey south to Florida.

Comments: This graceful, small tree blooms in early April on the visitors center nature trail in Great Smoky Mountains National Park, Tennessee, and along the roads in Fort Mountain State Park, Georgia.

Fringe Tree

Showy Orchis

SHOWY ORCHIS
Orchis spectabilis
Orchid Family (Orchidaceae)

Description: The large, ovate, shiny leaves are at the base of this 6–10" plant. The 1–1½" flowers are purple and white and have a white lip. Usually, several flowers bloom on the plant at one time.

Bloom Season: April–June

Habitat/Range: In rich, wooded areas from New Brunswick to Ontario and south to Georgia, Kentucky, Missouri, and Nebraska.

Comments: Because this plant is often 6" tall, it is a little harder to spot than its larger orchid cousins the Lady's Slippers. It starts to bloom in mid-April in southern locations such as the Chattahoochee National Forest in Georgia and mid- to late May on Blue Mountain in Virginia. It often grows at the edge of woodland trails at the base of a big tree.

Nodding Ladies Tresses

NODDING LADIES TRESSES
Spiranthes cernua
Orchid Family (Orchidaceae)

Description: The lanceolate, grasslike leaves are at the base of this 6–20" plant. The ½" flowers are white and hooded, and bend toward the ground.

Bloom Season: July–September

Habitat/Range: In wet grasses and open places from Quebec to Minnesota and South Dakota, and south to Texas and Florida.

Comments: There is a field of Nodding Ladies Tresses around mile 200 of the Blue Ridge Parkway that is usually in full bloom in September. Nodding Ladies Tresses are the most common of the small white orchids of the Southern Appalachian Mountains, but there are several others. Two other fairly common white orchids are Slender Ladies Tresses *(Spiranthes vernalis),* which blooms in the spring and has flowers forming a spiral around the stem, and Large Round-Leaved Orchid *(Planthera orbiculata),* which grows in the forest and has 2 large, flat, almost round base leaves.

COMMON WOOD SORREL
Oxalis montana
Wood-Sorrel Family (Oxalidaceae)

Description: The leaves, at the base of this 2–6" plant, are divided into 3 ovate leaflets that fold in half when the sun is not shining. The 1" flowers have 5 white petals with pink lines.

Bloom Season: May–August

Habitat/Range: In northern, cool, wooded areas and south to Pennsylvania. Also found in the Great Smoky Mountains at higher elevations.

Common Wood Sorrel

Comments: This is another plant that grows at the upper elevations of Great Smoky Mountains National Park and is normally only seen at altitudes above 2,000' in northern Pennsylvania and in the northern section of the Appalachian Mountains around Franconia, New Hampshire, and in the Adirondack Mountains of New York State.

SQUIRREL CORN
Dicentra canadensis
Poppy Family (Papaveraceae)

Description: The finely divided leaves are at the base of this 6–10" plant. The ½" flowers are white or faintly pink.

Bloom Season: April–May

Habitat/Range: In woods from Nova Scotia to Minnesota and south to North Carolina and Kansas.

Comments: Another common name for this plant is White Heart because of its shape. Sometimes it is mistaken for Dutchman's Breeches *(Dicentra cucullaria),* another plant of the poppy family found in many areas of the Southern Appalachian Mountains. Dutchman's Breeches looks like Squirrel Corn that has been hung upside down with its pant legs flaring on the bottom and the waistband on the top.

Squirrel Corn

Bloodroot

BLOODROOT
Sanguinaria canadensis
Poppy Family (Papaveraceae)

Description: The leaves have 5–9 lobes and are at the base of this 4–8" plant, usually after the flower has faded. The 1–1½" white flowers have 8–12 petals. When the flowers on the plant are in bloom, the leaf usually wraps around the stem of the plant.

Bloom Season: March–May

Habitat/Range: In rich wooded areas from Nova Scotia to Manitoba and south to Florida and Arkansas.

Comments: The plants bloom for about 1 week, depending on latitude and elevation. In low elevations in southern locations, it blooms in March, and in high elevations it blooms in May. When the flowers fade, this very distinctive leaf opens up and can be spotted on hillsides and banks all summer, marking the place where the plants will bloom in the spring. The thick rootstock, once used to produce a bright red dye, is poisonous if eaten.

Pokeweed

POKEWEED
Phytolacca americana
Pokeweed Family (Phytolaccaceae)

Description: The lanceolate leaves alternate on the stem of this 4–10' plant. The ¼" greenish white flowers form a long, loose cluster. Flower clusters and berries are often seen on the same plant.

Bloom Season: July–October

Habitat/Range: In both shaded and open areas from Maine and Ontario to Minnesota and south to Florida and Texas.

Comments: The root of the plant is poisonous. The young shoots are eaten like asparagus. The seeds are black or dark purple and possibly poisonous to humans. Birds love the berries and spread the plant far and wide.

VIRGINIA SPRING BEAUTY
Claytonia virginica
Purslane Family (Portulacaceae)

Description: Two long, lanceolate leaves are opposite each other on the stem of this 3–7" plant. The ½–¾", 5-petal flowers are white with pink lines. Sometimes there are so many lines the flower looks pink.

Bloom Season: March–May

Habitat/Range: In moist wooded areas from Nova Scotia to Saskatchewan and south to Georgia, Montana, and Texas.

Comments: Carolina Spring Beauty *(Claytonia caroliniana)* resembles Virginia Spring Beauty, but the leaves are wider. Both plants are commonly found in the Southern Appalachian Mountains. In April, Spring Beauties often carpet large areas beneath deciduous trees whose leaves are still not out.

Virginia Spring Beauty

Enchanter's Nightshade

ENCHANTER'S NIGHTSHADE
Circaea quadrisulcata
Primrose Family (Primulaceae)

Description: The toothed, ovate leaves are opposite each other on the stem of this 1–2' plant. The tiny flowers have 2 white petals and are in spikes with spaces between the flowers.

Bloom Season: June–August

Habitat/Range: In rich woods and thickets from Nova Scotia to Ontario and North Dakota south to Oklahoma, Tennessee, and Georgia.

Comments: The ancient Greeks described this as a magical herb and called it *circaea* or *kirkaia,* after the enchantress Circe. It is neither a true nightshade (which belong to the family Solanaceae) nor magical or enchanting. This plant, also called Bindweed-Nightshade or Mandrake, is a very common blooming plant along the trails of summer woodlands.

Shooting-Star

SHOOTING-STAR
Dodecatheon meadia
Primrose Family (Primulaceae)

Description: The lanceolate, entire leaves are at the base of this 8–18" plant. The 1½–2" flowers have 4 white, pink, or lilac petals that form a pointed, downward facing cone.

Bloom Season: April–May

Habitat/Range: On moist cliffs from Pennsylvania to Manitoba and south to Georgia and Texas.

Comments: Shooting-Star grows in the southwestern portion of the Appalachian Mountain Range (Tennessee and southwestern Virginia) in areas that have large amounts of rainfall like Great Smoky Mountains National Park. The plants often grow along stream banks.

WOOD ANEMONE OR WINDFLOWER
Anemone quinquefolia
Buttercup Family (Ranunculaceae)

Wood Anemone or Windflower

Description: The leaves are divided into 3–5 toothed leaflets and form a whorl on the stem of this 3–6" plant. The 1" flowers have 5 white or pinkish, petal-like sepals.

Bloom Season: March–May

Habitat/Range: A common woodland plant from the Atlantic Coastal Plain to the eastern mountains.

Comments: Early spring in the Appalachian Mountains moves north from week to week. Groups of Wood Anemone can be found along the roadsides in the Great Smoky Mountains National Park in late April, on the Appalachian Trail around Milam Gap, Shenandoah National Park, in early May, and on the Escarpment Trail at North Lake in the Catskill Mountains in late May.

Tall Anemone or Thimbleweed

TALL ANEMONE OR THIMBLEWEED
Anemone virginiana
Buttercup Family (Ranunculaceae)

Description: The toothed, lobed leaves are opposite each other on the stem of this 2–3' plant. The leaves are heavily veined. The 1–1½" flowers have 5 greenish white sepals that appear to be the flowers' petals.

Bloom Season: May–September

Habitat/Range: In rocky or dry, open wooded areas and along trails from Maine to North Dakota and south to Kansas, Arkansas, Alabama, and Georgia.

Comments: Native Americans used the liquid from the cooked roots to treat diarrhea and whooping cough. A poultice made from the root was a treatment for boils. Tall Anemone grows around mile 90 of the Virginia section of the Blue Ridge Parkway.

Rue Anemone

RUE ANEMONE
Anemonella thalictroides
Buttercup Family (Ranunculaceae)

Description: Three leaves, each with 3 lobes, form a whorl on the stem below the flower cluster of this 6–8" plant. The ¼–½" flowers are white or pinkish with 5–10 petal-like sepals.

Bloom Season: April–June

Habitat/Range: Found in open wooded areas from New Hampshire to Florida.

Comments: Rue Anemone is a very common plant in mid-April along trails and roadsides in Great Smoky Mountains National Park, along the Blue Ridge Parkway, in Chattahoochee National Forest, Georgia, and Fort Desoto State Park in Alabama.

BLACK COHOSH OR BLACK SNAKEROOT
Cimicifuga racemosa
Buttercup Family (Ranunculaceae)

Description: The leaves, which alternate on the stem of this 3–8' plant, are divided into many groups of 3 sharply toothed and lobed leaflets. The tiny, white flowers appear to be all stamens. The flowers form dense clusters on a long stalk.

Bloom Season: June–August

Habitat/Range: In open and wooded areas from western Massachusetts to Southern Ontario and south as far as Georgia, Tennessee, and Missouri.

Comments: As summer progresses large colonies of Black Snakeroot start blooming throughout the Southern Appalachian Mountains from the Blue Ridge Parkway south. In July at the northern border of the region on the Blue Ridge, it is not unusual to see numerous plants at the edge of Skyline Drive and in the woods. Another species that looks very much like Black Snakeroot, Bugbane *(Cimicifuga americana)*, grows in the mountains of West Virginia. Bugbane does not get as tall and has several pistils in each flower.

Black Cohosh or Black Snakeroot

VIRGIN'S BOWER
Clematis virginiana
Buttercup Family (Ranunculaceae)

Description: The leaves on this vine are divided into 3 toothed leaflets. The 1" white flowers have 4 petals. The fruit is a cluster of feathery hairs called Old Man's Beard.

Bloom Season: July–September

Habitat/Range: A long vine climbing over bushes and along streams and rivers from Nova Scotia to Georgia.

Comments: Found on Chestnut Hill on the Tennessee side of Great Smoky Mountains National Park. Some people develop skin rashes if they touch this plant.

Virgin's Bower

Goldenseal or Orangeroot

GOLDENSEAL OR ORANGEROOT
Hydrastis canadensis
Buttercup Family (Ranunculaceae)

Description: The maple-shaped leaves alternate on the stem of this 8–15" plant. The ½" white flowers are composed of a tuft of stamens.

Bloom Season: May

Habit/Range: In wooded areas from Vermont to Minnesota and south to Georgia, Alabama, and Arkansas.

Comments: This is a popular plant in folk medicine because it contains the antibacterial berberine. Unfortunately, it has become less common in some eastern deciduous forests because of excessive harvesting.

Waxy Meadow Rue

WAXY MEADOW RUE
Thalictrum revolutum
Buttercup Family (Ranunculaceae)

Description: The leaves alternate on the stem of this 2–6' plant and are divided into lobed leaflets. The flowers have 4 small white petals with extended, drooping stamens.

Bloom Season: May–June

Habitat/Range: On rocky, wooded slopes and sometimes in meadows from Massachusetts to Ontario and south to South Carolina and Missouri.

Comments: Early Meadow Rue *(Thalictrum dioicum)* also grows in the same habitat in the Appalachian Mountains, but it blooms about one month earlier than Waxy Meadow Rue. The plant is very similar in appearance, but the flowers are greenish yellow, and the drooping stamens are smaller than those of Waxy Meadow Rue.

NEW JERSEY TEA
Ceanothus americanus
Buckthorn Family (Rhamnaceae)

Description: The ovate, toothed leaves alternate on the stem of this 1½–3' shrub. The ¼" white flowers have 5 petals and form long clusters.

Bloom Season: June–September

Habitat/Range: In dry open woods and on rocky banks from Maine to Ontario and south to Florida and Texas.

Comments: Tea made from the leaves of New Jersey Tea was once a popular beverage. Native Americans made a tea from the root of the plant and used it to aid in the cure of a large number of ailments, including the common cold. The root of the plant is strongly astringent.

New Jersey Tea

Goatsbeard

GOATSBEARD
Aruncus dioicus
Rose Family (Rosaceae)

Description: The leaves are divided into 5 ovate, toothed leaflets. The tiny flowers have 5 white petals and form a long, slender cluster on the branch of this 3–6' shrub.

Bloom Season: May–July

Habitat/Range: Leaning out over back roads and streams or erect in rich woods from Pennsylvania to Iowa and south to Georgia and Missouri.

Comments: False Goatsbeard *(Astible biternata)*, a plant of the Saxifrage family, can easily be mistaken for Goatsbeard. Unlike Goatsbeard, False Goatsbeard has a 3-lobed terminal leaflet. Goatsbeard *(Aruncus dioicus)* has plants with male flowers and separate plants with female flowers. The male flowers have 5 white petals and 15–20 white stamens. The female flower has 3 pistils at its center but also has non-functioning stamen. Goatsbeards grow along Rich Mountain Road in Great Smoky Mountains National Park.

Common Strawberry or Wild Strawberry

COMMON STRAWBERRY OR WILD STRAWBERRY
Fragaria virginiana
Rose Family (Rosaceae)

Description: The leaves, divided into 3 sharply toothed, ovate leaflets, are at the base of this 2–6" plant. The ½–¾", white flowers have 5 petals.

Bloom Season: April–July

Habitat/Range: In dry soils from Newfoundland to Alberta and south to Georgia, Alabama, and Oklahoma

Comments: The small red fruit is edible and juicy, but it takes a lot of picking to make a pie. The plant is a very common ground cover in woods as well as in dry meadows.

COMMON NINEBARK
Physocarpus opulifolius
Rose Family (Rosaceae)

Description: The 3 lobed, ¾–3"-long, toothed leaves alternate on the stem of this 3–10' shrub. The ¼" flowers have 5 pink or white petals and form an umbel.

Bloom Season: May–June

Habitat/Range: On riverbanks and in rocky places from Maine to Georgia.

Comments: To see the wonderful displays of flowering shrubs, take a drive in the Southern Appalachian Mountains in late May and early June. Many of the blooming shrubs can be seen while slowly driving along the roads, but Ninebark's beautiful pink and white umbels probably will not be noticed without taking a walk along a trail.

Common Ninebark

Common Blackberry

COMMON BLACKBERRY
Rubus alleghaniensis
Rose Family (Rosaceae)

Description: The divided and toothed leaves do not appear at flowering time on the 2–4' woody stems. The ½–1" white flowers have 5 petals.

Bloom Season: May–June

Habitat/Range: In dry soils from Nova Scotia to North Carolina.

Comments: Many varieties of blackberries grow in the Southern Appalachian Mountains. In Great Smoky Mountains National Park, blackberries are found at the lower elevations. The fruit ripens in August and September.

Wine Raspberry or Wineberry

WINE RASPBERRY OR WINEBERRY
Rubus phoenicolasius
Rose Family (Rosaceae)

Description: The leaves are made up of 3 heart-shaped, toothed leaflets that have a silvery undersurface and purplish veins. The leaves alternate on the stem of this 1–4' plant. The stems of the shrub are red, bristly, and sparsely prickly. The ½" flowers have 5 small, white petals. The fruit is red.

Bloom Season: May–June

Habitat/Range: Escaped from cultivation, it has spread easily into meadows and the edges of roads and woods. This shrub is native to eastern Asia.

Comments: The plant is invasive and often takes over a natural habitat. It is used ornamentally because of its foliage. It spreads easily because wherever the stem of the plant touches the ground it will form a new root. The berries are edible, but not as tasty as our native raspberry.

BUTTON BUSH
Cephalanthus occidentalis
Madder Family (Rubiaceae)

Description: The egg-shaped leaves are opposite each other on the stem of this 2–10' plant. The ¼" tubular flowers have 5 white petals and form a ball.

Bloom Season: June–July

Habitat/Range: In wet places from Nova Scotia to southern Ontario, Minnesota, and California, and south to Texas and Florida.

Comments: Also called Honeyballs; in some cases cultivated as an ornamental shrub. It grows in Great Smoky Mountains National Park at low elevations.

Button Bush

Wild Madder

WILD MADDER
Galium mollugo
Madder Family (Rubiaceae)

Description: The 7–8 entire, lanceolate leaves whorl around the stem of this 8–18" plant. The tiny flowers have 4 white petals and form big clusters.

Bloom Season: May–August

Habitat/Range: In fields and meadows from Newfoundland to Ontario and south to Virginia and Tennessee.

Comments: This European plant has been widely naturalized. The genus name *Galium* comes from the Greek word for milk, *gala*. Many of the plants of this genus were used to curdle milk in the cheese-making process. The pleasant scent from the dried plants of this genus comes from the chemical coumarin, related to the modern synthetic chemical (dicoumarin) used as a blood-thinning agent.

Bastard Toadflax or Star Toadflax

BASTARD TOADFLAX OR STAR TOADFLAX

Comandra umbellata
Sandalwood Family (Santalaceae)

Description: The oblong leaves alternate on the stem of this 6–15' parasitic plant. The ⅛" greenish white flowers are in the shape of a bell. Each flower has 5 lobed calyxes that appear to be petals.

Bloom Season: May

Habitat/Range: In dry, wooded areas and fields from Maine west to Michigan and south to Georgia and Alabama.

Comments: The underground rhizome of the plants of the genus *Comandra* feed parasitically off the roots of a number of woody plants. Bastard Toadflax is mostly found in the Midwest. It also grows in a few of the mountainous counties of North Carolina.

LIZARD'S TAIL OR WATER DRAGON

Saururus cernuus
Lizard Tail Family (Saururaceae)

Description: The heart-shaped leaves alternate on the stem of this 1–3' plant. The 4–6" flowers are white and in terminal spikes. The spikes can be up to 8" and are usually curved.

Bloom Season: June–September

Habitat/Range: A plant of wet places such as swamps, wetlands, and shallow water found from Maine west to Minnesota and south to Florida and Texas.

Comments: Also called Swamp Dragon or Breast Weed, the root was used by some Native Americans in a poultice to treat wounds and inflamed breasts. The colonists adopted it and its use was documented in mid-18th century herbal medicine literature. This plant has no petals or sepals. The color of the flower comes about because that part of the stamen that holds no pollen is white.

Lizard's Tail or Water Dragon

MITERWORT OR BISHOP'S CAP
Mitella diphylla
Saxifrage Family (Saxifragaceae)

Description: The lobed, toothed, heart-shaped leaves are at the base of this 6–16" plant. The ¼" flowers have 5 petals that form a tiny, white, fringed bell.

Bloom Season: March–June

Habitat/Range: In rich wooded areas from Quebec to Minnesota and south to North Carolina and Missouri.

Comments: This plant is also called Fairy-cup because of its very pretty fringed flowers. It is the type of flower whose beauty is best appreciated through a magnifying glass.

Miterwort or Bishop's Cap

Grass-of-Parnassus

GRASS-OF-PARNASSUS
Parnassia asarifolia
Saxifrage Family (Saxifragaceae)

Descriptions: The heart-shaped, fleshy leaves are at the base of this 6–20" plant. The flowers are about 1" wide with 5 white petals. Each petal has thin lines from the tip of the petal to the center of the flower. The lines are green at first and turn brown as the flower ages.

Bloom Season: July–October

Habitat/Range: Found in wet places from southwest Virginia to the Great Smoky Mountains.

Comments: The small, wet shelves in the rock faces that line sections of the Blue Ridge Parkway in North Carolina are an excellent place to look for this flower.

Brook Lettuce

BROOK LETTUCE
Saxifraga micranthidifolia
Saxifrage Family (Saxifragaceae)

Description: The long, lanceolate leaves are at the base of this 12–30" plant. The ½" white flowers have 5 petals.

Bloom Season: April–May

Habitat/Range: In wet places from southern Pennsylvania to the Great Smoky Mountains.

Comments: This plant grows in wet places near the road and along the streams that run under the road that loops through Cades Cove, Great Smoky Mountains National Park, Tennessee.

FOAMFLOWER OR FALSE MITERWORT
Tiarella cordifolia
Saxifrage Family (Saxifragaceae)

Description: The lobed and toothed leaves are at the base of this 6–12" plant. The ½" flowers have 5 white petals. The flowers grow on the top portion of the plant's stem and form a small pyramid.

Bloom Season: April–June

Habitat/Range: In rich, moist, wooded areas from Nova Scotia to Minnesota and south to eastern Alabama and western Georgia, especially in the mountains.

Comments: This plant blooms in Fort Mountain State Park in Georgia from mid-April and the White Mountains of New Hampshire in late June.

Foamflower or False Miterwort

Foxglove Beardtongue or White Beardtongue

FOXGLOVE BEARDTONGUE OR WHITE BEARDTONGUE

Penstemon digitalis

Snapdragon Family (Scrophulariaceae)

Description: The lanceolate, toothed leaves are stalkless and opposite each other on the stem of this 2–4' plant. The 1½–2" white or purple-tinged flowers have 5 petals and are trumpet shaped and swollen in the middle. The flowers form a cluster at the top of the plant.

Bloom Season: June–August

Habitat/Range: In fields and thickets from Maine to Tennessee and from Illinois and Kansas to Arkansas.

Comments: In some western places, people believed this plant grew more often on graves and called it Dead-Men's Bells. Other beard-tongues, such as Hairy Beardtongue *(Penstemon canescens),* which looks a lot like Foxglove Beardtongue, but its trumpet-shaped flower is not swollen in the middle, also grow in the Southern Appalachian Mountains.

Moth Mullein

MOTH MULLEIN
Verbascum blattaria
Snapdragon Family (Scrophulariaceae)

Description: The toothed, stemless, smooth leaves alternate on the lower part of the stem of this 2–5' plant. The ¾–1" flowers are on the upper part of the stem and have 5 yellow or white petals and 5 prominent red stamens in the center of the flower.

Bloom Season: June–October

Habitat/Range: In fields and at the edge of woods practically throughout the United States.

Comments: Colonists introduced Moth Mullein to the United States from Europe. The plant gets its common name because the flowers seem to imitate all the parts of a moth, with the lower 3 hairy stamens as the tongue.

CULVER'S ROOT
Veronicastrum virginicum
Snapdragon Family (Scrophulariaceae)

Description: The toothed, lanceolate leaves form a whorl on the stem of this 2–7' plant. The tiny, 4-petal, white flowers form spikes.

Bloom Season: June–September

Habitat/Range: In wooded areas and meadows in New England and from Virginia south to Alabama and Arkansas. Also found in Texas.

Comments: This plant contains a drug that works on the digestive system. Native Americans made a tea from the dried roots to treat a variety of complaints. The fresh root is potentially toxic.

Culver's Root

Silver Bell Tree or Snow Drop Tree

SILVER BELL TREE OR SNOW DROP TREE
Halesia carolina
Storax Family (Styracaceae)

Description: The stalked, pointed, ovate leaves do not appear at flowering time on this usually small (around 5') streamside shrub or tree. The 1–1½", white, 5-petal flowers are bell shaped.

Bloom Season: April–May

Habitat/Range: In rich, moist, wooded areas and along stream banks from Virginia and West Virginia to Ohio, Kentucky, and Illinois, and south to Florida, Alabama, and Tennessee.

Comments: Also called Opossumwood, this beautiful small tree blossoms in April along the Newfound Gap Road (US 441) and along the Little River Road between Sugarlands and Elkmont in Great Smoky Mountains National Park. In these locations the trees are their usual size, no more than 5', but there are some very large Silver Bell Trees in the park.

Queen Anne's Lace or Wild Carrot

QUEEN ANNE'S LACE OR WILD CARROT
Daucus carota
Parsley Family (Umbelliferae)

Description: The finely divided leaves alternate on the stem of this 2–3' plant. The tiny flowers have 5 white petals, and there is often 1 dark purple or black center flower in the 4–6" umbel the white flowers form. There are rare groups of Queen Anne's Lace with pink flowers.

Bloom Season: May–October

Habitat/Range: On roadsides and in open places throughout North America.

Comments: In some places in North America, this beautiful plant is a pest because it propagates so easily and takes over entire areas. The edible carrot is the root of an Asian relative of this plant. The root of Queen Anne's Lace is white.

COW PARSNIP
Heracleum maximum
Parsley Family (Umbelliferae)

Description: The large, maplelike leaves alternate and clasp the stem of this 3–6' plant. The tiny, 5-petal flowers are white and form a large, flat cluster.

Bloom Season: June–September

Habitat/Range: In moist and rich soils from Newfoundland to Alaska and south to Florida and California.

Comments: Native Americans used a tea from the root of this plant to cure a variety of complaints. The foliage is poisonous to livestock and the sap can cause skin irritations. Be careful touching or using plants of the parsley family, as some are extremely poisonous.

Cow Parsnip

ANISEROOT OR LONG-STYLES SWEET CICELY
Osmorhiza longistylis
Parsley Family (Umbelliferae)

Aniseroot or Long-Styles Sweet Cicely

Description: The fernlike leaves alternate on the stem of this 1–3' woodland plant. The ⅛" white flowers have 5 petals and form small umbels. The styles of the flower protrude beyond the petals.

Bloom Season: May–June

Habitat/Range: In wooded areas throughout the eastern United States.

Comments: The root of the plant has the shape of a carrot and smells like licorice. Native Americans used the plant medicinally. In early April Aniseroot blooms along the Sugarlands Visitors Center Nature Trail in Great Smoky Mountains National Park, Tennessee.

Cowbane

COWBANE
Oxypolis rigidior
Parsley Family (Umbelliferae)

Description: The leaves are divided into opposite, sparsely toothed, narrow, lanceolate leaflets. The leaves alternate on the stem of this 2–6' plant. The tiny, 5-petal, white flowers form flat clusters.

Bloom Season: August–September

Habitat/Range: In swamps and wet woods from New York to Minnesota and south to Florida and Texas.

Comments: This plant is poisonous. Many parsley family (Umbelliferae) plants with 5-petal, white flowers that form a flat cluster are poisonous. It is best to be wary of using any part of these plants for any purpose except decoration.

White Vervain

WHITE VERVAIN
Verbena urticifolia
Vervain Family (Verbenaceae)

Description: The toothed, lanceolate leaves are opposite each other on the stem of this 2–5' plant. The tiny, white flowers form an interrupted spike.

Bloom Season: June–September

Habitat/Range: In fields from New Brunswick to South Dakota and south to Texas and Florida.

Comments: The English name of this plant seems to be an Anglicized version of the Latin word *verbena*. In classical Rome, a verbena was a sacred herb or branch carried in ceremonies.

SWEET WHITE VIOLET
Viola blanda
Violet Family (Violacaea)

Description: The toothed, ovate leaves are at the base of this 4–6" plant and grow on a separate stem from the flowers. The ½" flowers have 5 white petals. The petals are placed 2 at the top of the flower and 3 at the bottom.

Bloom Season: March–June

Habitat/Range: In rich places from Quebec to Minnesota south to Maryland and the mountains of Georgia and Tennessee.

Comments: Sweet White Violet can be found in early April in the Beartree Recreation Area of the Jefferson National Forest in Virginia.

Sweet White Violet

CANADA VIOLET
Viola canadensis
Violet Family (Violacaea)

Description: The toothed, heart-shaped leaves alternate on the stem of this 4–8" plant. The ½–1" white flowers have a yellow throat. Each flower has 5 petals.

Bloom Season: March–June

Habitat/Range: In mountains and wooded uplands from Newfoundland to eastern British Columbia in the Rockies, and south to Arizona, New Mexico, and Alabama.

Comments: Violets bloom in several colors and grow either as plants with base leaves on a separate stem from the flowers or as does the Canada Violet, with the leaves and the flower on the same stem. Canada Violets can be found on the Chimney Top Nature Trail in Great Smoky Mountains National Park and in the Fort Mountain State Park in Georgia.

Canada Violet

Field Pansy

FIELD PANSY
Viola kitaibeliana
Violet Family (Violacaea)

Description: The spoon-shaped leaves are opposite each other on the stem of this 4–6" plant. The ½–¾" white flower has 5 petals. Each petal has thin, purple stripes radiating from a bright yellow center.

Bloom Season: April–May

Habitat/Range: Along roads and in meadows from New York to Iowa and south to Georgia and Texas.

Comments: Field Pansies are quite small and their pastel colors sometimes serve as camouflage, hiding them in the early spring grass. They usually grow in large groups, and although delicate, they are so pretty that they definitely deserve a close-up look. They can be found along the Blue Ridge Parkway as early as the beginning of April.

YELLOW FLOWERS

Prickly Pear

Yellow Stargrass

YELLOW STARGRASS
Hypoxis hirsuta
Amaryllis Family (Amaryllidaceae)

Description: The grasslike leaves are at the base of this 3–6" plant. The ½–¾" yellow flowers form a star.

Bloom Season: April–September

Habitat/Range: In dry soils in meadows and open, wooded areas from Maine to Manitoba and south to Florida and Texas.

Comments: There is often a cluster of flowers, and their bright yellow stars light up a woodland glen in the forests of the Appalachian Mountains. Start to look for them in early April at the Sosebee Cove area of Chattahoochee National Forest and the Fort Mountain State Park, both in Georgia.

SKUNK CABBAGE
Symplocarpus foetidus
Arum Family (Araceae)

Description: The very large, egg-shaped leaves are a familiar sight in wet places, but there are none at flowering time on this 12–18" plant. The 6–8" red, often mottled hood (spathe) surrounds a knob-shaped cluster of yellow flowers (spadix).

Bloom Season: February–May

Habitat/Range: In wet and swampy places from Nova Scotia to Minnesota and south to North Carolina and Iowa.

Comments: When the Skunk Cabbage starts blooming in February, sometimes pushing up through snow and ice, it often goes unnoticed. What is noticed in swampy areas are the huge leaves that give this plant its name. When a leaf is broken, it emits a foul odor.

Skunk Cabbage

VICTOR MEDINA

Pale Jewelweed or Pale Touch-Me-Not

PALE JEWELWEED OR PALE TOUCH-ME-NOT
Impatiens pallida
Jewelweed Family (Balsaminaceae)

Description: The egg-shaped, slightly toothed leaves alternate on the stem of this 1–5' plant. The petals of the 1–2" yellow flowers form a tilted cup with a lip.

Bloom Season: June–September

Habitat/Range: In damp woods and thickets, particularly near streams, from Quebec to Saskatchewan and south to North Carolina, Tennessee, and Missouri.

Comments: Less common than Orange Jewelweed *(Impatiens capensis),* the yellow Jewelweed grows in large quantities in many locations in the Southern Appalachian Mountains. Look for Pale Jewelweed in the Mount Rogers Recreation area of the Jefferson National Forest in Virginia and in Great Smoky Mountains National Park at Newfound Gap, the Green Briar Picnic Area, and along the roadsides.

Early Winter Cress

EARLY WINTER CRESS
Barbarea verna
Mustard Family (Brassicaceae)

Description: The leaves at the base of the plant have 8–20 lobes, with a round terminal lobe. The stem leaves alternate on this 1–2' plant. The ¼–½" flowers have 4 yellow petals. The flowers form small clusters.

Bloom Season: March–May

Habitat/Range: In open places from Massachusetts to Southern New York; also in the Southern Appalachian Mountains and on the West Coast.

Comment: In some areas Early Winter Cress is cultivated as a salad green. It grows at low elevations in Great Smoky Mountains National Park.

PRICKLY PEAR
Opuntia humifusa
Cactus Family (Cactaceae)

Description: The broad, flattened stems called pads contain small tufts of evenly spaced bristles. The 2–3" flowers have many yellow petals that are integrated with yellow sepals.

Bloom Season: May–June

Habitat/Range: Open sandy or rocky areas from Massachusetts to Minnesota and south to Georgia.

Comments: Unlike many other cactus plants, Prickly Pear does not have spines. However, the small tufts of bristles on the flattened pads detach themselves when something brushes against them. If their barbs hit bare flesh it can be very painful. Prickly Pears grow throughout the Southern Appalachian Mountains, but are not common.

Prickly Pear

NODDING BUR MARIGOLD

Bidens cernua

Composite Family (Compositae)

Nodding Bur Marigold

Description: The toothed, long and narrow, lanceolate leaves are opposite each other on the stem of this 1–6' plant. The 1–1½" yellow flowers have 6–8 often reflexed petals surrounding a disk.

Bloom Season: August–October

Habitat/Range: From Nova Scotia to Hudson Bay and British Columbia and south to North Carolina. Also found in California.

Comments: *Bidens* are also called Beggar Ticks. They get their name because the seeds they produce adhere to the surface of anything that brushes against them. The seed covers have 2 sharp barbs that stick to hikers' clothing like ticks. This is the way these plants spread their seeds and propagate in new locations. Another bur marigold *(Bidens laevis),* which also grows in the Southern Appalachians, can be found in the Cades Cove area of Great Smoky Mountains National Park.

Green and Gold or Goldenstar

GREEN AND GOLD OR GOLDENSTAR

Chrysogonum virginianum

Composite Family (Compositae)

Description: The ovate, toothed leaves are opposite each other on the stem of this 3–12" plant. The 1–2" flowers have 5 yellow, rounded petals.

Bloom Season: April–July

Habitat/Range: In dry soils from southern Pennsylvania to Alabama.

Comments: When Green and Gold starts blooming in early spring, the plant is 3–4" high. When it blooms in summer, it is often 1' or more. It grows mostly on the Piedmont and the Coastal Plains in the central Atlantic states and at low altitudes in the Alabama and Georgia mountains.

Grass-Leaved Golden Aster

GRASS-LEAVED GOLDEN ASTER
Chrysopsis graminifolia
Composite Family (Compositae)

Description: The grasslike leaves of this 1–2' plant are wider at the base of the plant than those on the stem. The ½–1" yellow flowers have many petals and a center yellow disk.

Bloom Season: July–September

Habitat/Range: In dry soils from Delaware to Florida.

Comments: This golden aster can be found in Tallulah Gorge State Park in Georgia. The Maryland Golden Aster or Broad-Leaved Golden Aster *(Chrysopsis mariana)* has spoon-shaped leaves and larger petals and can be found along the Blue Ridge Parkway in North Carolina.

EARED COREOPSIS OR LITTLE EARS
Coreopsis auricalata
Composite Family (Compositae)

Description: The lanceolate leaves seem to have small, round ears, hence its name, and are at the base of this 6–10" plant. The 1–1½" flowers have 6–8 yellow notched petals.

Bloom Season: April–June

Habitat/Range: In wooded areas from Virginia to Illinois and south to Kentucky and Florida.

Comments: Unlike other coreopsis found in the Southern Appalachian Mountains, Little Ears are not found any further north. Little Ears can be found at low altitudes in Great Smoky Mountains National Park.

Eared Coreopsis or Little Ears

Garden Tickseed or Golden Coreopsis

GARDEN TICKSEED OR GOLDEN COREOPSIS

Coreopsis tinctoria
Composite Family (Compositae)

Description: The leaves are divided into 2–3 grasslike leaflets and are opposite each other on the stem of this 1–3' plant. The 1½–2" yellow petal flowers have brown splashes around the center of the flower.

Bloom Season: June–September

Habitat/Range: In moist soils from Minnesota to Alberta.

Comments: The plant escaped from gardens in the eastern part of the United States and can be found in the Great Smoky Mountains.

Tall Coreopsis

TALL COREOPSIS
Coreopsis tripteris
Composite Family (Compositae)

Description: The leaves, divided into 3 entire and stemless leaflets, are opposite each other on the stem of this 1½–3' plant. The 2–3" flowers have 8 or more yellow petals.

Bloom Season: July–September

Habitat/Range: In moist soils from Kansas and Missouri south to Texas and east to Georgia.

Comments: Tall Coreopsis is found in the Great Smoky Mountains in the Newtown Gap area and around milepost 200 on the Blue Ridge Parkway in North Carolina. A similar plant, Large Coreopsis or Greater Coreopsis *(Coreopsis major)*, is also a prominent plant and one of the showiest of the wild coreopsis in the Southern Appalachian Mountains because its petals are often double and the disk is brown.

SNEEZEWEED
Helenium autumnale
Composite Family (Compositae)

Description: The toothed stem leaves extend down the stem, forming wings. The leaves alternate on the stem of this 2–6' plant. The 1–2" yellow flowers have wedge–shaped petals, and the center disk is yellow and knob shaped.

Bloom Season: July–October

Habitat/Range: In moist soils practically throughout the United States and southern Canada.

Comments: Sneezeweeds get their name from a practice of Native Americans who sniffed a powder made of dried, nearly mature flower heads as a cure for colds. Sneezeweed can be found around mile 200 of the Blue Ridge Parkway in North Carolina.

Sneezeweed

PURPLE-HEADED SNEEZEWEED
Helenium nudiflorum
Composite Family (Compositae)

Description: The stem leaves are entire or have a few teeth and extend down the stem, forming wings. The leaves alternate on the stem of this 1–3' plant. The 1–1½" flowers have wedge-shaped yellow petals and a brown or purple knob-shaped disk.

Bloom Season: June–October

Habitat/Range: In open places and on roadsides, a native of the southern United States introduced into the northern states.

Comments: Some individuals are allergic to sneezeweed pollen. Some of the sneezeweeds are toxic to cattle. Another plant called Bitterweed *(Helenium anurum),* with threadlike leaves and many flowers that look like a smaller version of the 2 sneezeweeds illustrated here, also grows in the Southern Appalachian Mountains.

Purple-Headed Sneezeweed

Common Sunflower

COMMON SUNFLOWER
Helianthus annuus
Composite Family (Compositae)

Description: The heart-shaped, rough, toothed leaves are placed singly on the stem of this 3–12' plant. The 3–5" yellow flowers have a brown disk.

Bloom Season: July–October

Habitat/Range: Found in open places and native to states from Minnesota to Idaho and south to Texas and California. Quite common in the northeastern states and found in river valleys and along roads in the Appalachian Mountains.

Comments: The flowers of the wild Common Sunflower are often less than half the size of the cultivated plant. The flowers yield a golden dye and the edible seeds are pressed to obtain a useful oil. The plants in the Appalachian Mountains might be the offspring of cultivated plants that have found their way back to the wild.

Thin-Leaved Sunflower

THIN-LEAVED SUNFLOWER
Helianthus decapetalus
Composite Family (Compositae)

Description: The toothed leaves are thin, the upper leaves are usually alternate, and the lower are opposite each other on the stem of this 2–5' plant. The 2–3" yellow flowers have a yellow disk and usually have 10 petals.

Bloom Season: July–September

Habitat/Range: In moist woods and along streams from Quebec to Michigan and south to Georgia, Tennessee, and Missouri.

Comments: There are about 70 species of sunflowers native to the New World and this is one of several varieties commonly found in the Appalachian Mountains. Thin-Leaved Sunflower is commonly found along the Blue Ridge Parkway in Virginia.

WOODLAND SUNFLOWER
Helianthus divaricatus
Composite Family (Compositae)

Description: The lanceolate, toothed leaves have a very short stalk and are opposite each other on the stem of this 2–5' plant. The leaves have a rounded, broad base and one main vein. The 2–4" flowers have 8–12 yellow petals and a yellow disk. The disk is about ½".

Bloom Season: July–September

Habitat/Range: In moist, wooded areas and along streams from Pennsylvania to Georgia and west to Ohio, Missouri, and Louisiana.

Comments: The Small Woodland Sunflower *(Helianthus microcephalus)* looks a good deal like its larger relative the Woodland Sunflower. The flowers of Small Woodland Sunflower can be as small as 1" wide, with a ¼" disk. Often there are 2 flowers on a stem and the leaves are tapered on both ends. The Small Woodland Sunflower grows along the Lake Trail in Hungry Mother State Park in Virginia and the

Woodland Sunflower

Woodland Sunflower can be found in the Mount Rogers Recreation Area of Jefferson National Forest in Virginia.

Tall or Giant Sunflower

TALL OR GIANT SUNFLOWER

Helianthus giganteus
Composite Family (Compositae)

Description: The toothed, lanceolate leaves alternate on the stem of this 4–10' plant. The 1–2" flowers have 10–20 yellow petals and a yellow disk.

Bloom Season: July–October

Habitat/Range: In wet places from Saskatchewan, Ontario, and Maine south to Florida.

Comments: The Tall Sunflowers found in the Southern Appalachian Mountains are usually about 10' tall. The 1–2" flowers look small on such a big plant. In September huge stands of this tall plant with bright yellow flowers can be seen along the Blue Ridge Parkway. Pale-Leaved Sunflowers *(Helianthus strumosus)* can also be found along the parkway. In contrast to the Tall Sunflower, Pale-Leaved Sunflowers are shorter, have between 6–8 petals, and their leaves are opposite each other on the stem.

Jerusalem Artichoke

JERUSALEM ARTICHOKE
Helianthus tuberosus
Composite Family (Compositae)

Description: The toothed, egg-shaped upper leaves alternate, but the lower leaves are usually opposite each other on the stem of this 6–10' plant. The leaves and stems are rough textured. The 2–3½" flowers are yellow.

Bloom Season: August–October

Habitat/Range: In thickets and fields from Saskatchewan, Ontario, and Maine south to Georgia and Arkansas.

Comments: The common name of this plant is odd because the plant has nothing to do with Jerusalem and no relationship to artichokes. Native Americans and colonists ate the tuber of this plant. It is sometimes available in supermarkets or specialty stores today.

KING DEVIL HAWKWEED OR FIELD HAWKWEED
Hieracium pratense
Composite Family (Compositae)

Description: The lanceolate, hairy leaves have some teeth and are at the base of this 1–2' plant. The stem is also hairy. The 1½" yellow, dandelionlike flowers grow in groups at the top of the plant.

Bloom Season: May–September

Habitat/Range: In meadows and by roadsides from Quebec and Ontario south to Georgia.

Comments: This hawkweed has been naturalized in eastern North America from Europe. Eastern North America has several different kinds of native hawkweeds. Often mistaken for a dandelion because of their squared rays, other hawkweeds in the Southern Appalachian Mountains are Mouse-eared Hawkweed *(Hieracium pilosella),* named for its hairy roseate of base leaves, and Rattlesnake Weed *(Hieracium venosum),* named for the distinct purple veins in its roseate of base leaves.

King Devil Hawkweed or Field Hawkweed

MOUNTAIN CYNTHIA
Krigia montana
Composite Family (Compositae)

Description: The lanceolate, toothed leaves are at the base of this 6–12" plant. The 1–1½" bright yellow flowers look something like a dandelion.

Bloom Season: May–September

Habitat/Range: On wet cliffs and rocky stream banks in the mountains south of Northern Virginia.

Comments: Like the hawkweeds, the cynthias are often mistaken for dandelions. Mountain Cynthia can be seen on the rocky, often dripping ledges that line the Blue Ridge Parkway in North Carolina.

Mountain Cynthia

Prairie or Gray-Headed Coneflower

PRAIRIE OR GRAY-HEADED CONEFLOWER
Ratibida pinnata
Composite Family (Compositae)

Description: The leaves, divided into 3–7 slender leaflets, alternate on the stem of this 3–6' plant. The 2–4" flowers have 7–10 reflexed yellow petals and a central disk that forms a tall knob.

Bloom Season: June–September

Habitat/Range: In fields and on prairies from Minnesota to western New York and south to Georgia, Arkansas, and Oklahoma.

Comments: The Prairie Coneflower, as the name suggests, was once most often seen on the prairies from Minnesota south, but they have moved eastward and are now fairly common in the Southern Appalachians and can be seen along the Blue Ridge Parkway. This coneflower is different from other coneflowers because the central cylindrical receptacle of the flower (which normally is called the disk) can be several inches long.

Black-Eyed Susan

BLACK-EYED SUSAN
Rudbeckia hirta
Composite Family (Compositae)

Description: The lanceolate, slightly toothed leaves alternate on the stem of this 1–3' plant. The leaves are hairy and thick. The 2–4" flowers have many yellow petals and a dark brown center disk.

Bloom Season: June–October

Habitat/Range: In meadows and on prairies, widely distributed in the eastern United States and in Canada from Quebec to Manitoba.

Comments: Growing in the Southern Appalachian Mountains in the fall is a plant whose range is from New Jersey south to North Carolina and Kentucky called Orange Coneflower *(Rudbeckia fulgida)*. From a distance, Orange Coneflowers look exactly like Black-Eyed Susans, but come closer and it is apparent that near the dark brown, center, knoblike disk, the petals are orange.

GREEN-HEADED CONEFLOWER OR TALL CONEFLOWER
Rudbeckia laciniata
Composite Family (Compositae)

Description: The toothed and divided leaves alternate on the stem of this 3–10' plant. The 3–4" flowers have slightly reflexed yellow petals and a knoblike green disk.

Bloom Season: August–September

Habitat/Range: In moist and rich soils from Quebec to Manitoba and south to Georgia, Arkansas, and Oklahoma.

Comments: A plant that is commonly found throughout the Appalachian Mountains, this stately coneflower can be seen growing along the Blue Ridge Parkway at many locations, including near its most northern entrance point in Virginia and around milepost 200 in North Carolina. It can also be found in the Deep Creek area of Great Smoky Mountains National Park.

Green-Headed Coneflower or Tall Coneflower

THIN-LEAVED CONEFLOWER
Rudbeckia triloba
Composite Family (Compositae)

Description: The lower leaves have 3 lobes and most of the stem leaves are lanceolate and toothed. The leaves alternate on the stem of this 2–4' plant. The 2–3" flowers have yellow petals and a brown disk.

Bloom Season: June–October

Habitat/Range: In open, wooded areas and thickets from New York to Minnesota and south to Florida, Louisiana, and Oklahoma.

Comments: Another plant that from a distance could be mistaken for a Black-Eyed Susan, this one is sometimes called a Three-Lobed Black-Eyed Susan. However, it is smaller, has fewer rays than *Rudbeckia hirta,* and is less hairy. Thin-Leaved Coneflower is less common than its cousin Black-Eyed Susan. It can be found in the Cades Cove and Chimney Top picnic areas of Great Smoky Mountains National Park.

Thin-Leaved Coneflower

Golden Ragwort

GOLDEN RAGWORT
Senecio aureus
Composite Family (Compositae)

Description: The stem leaves are finely divided and there is 1 heart-shaped leaf at the base of this 6–24" plant. The ½" flowers have 8–13 yellow petals and the disk is yellow.

Bloom Season: April–August

Habitat/Range: In wet soils from Newfoundland to Florida.

Comments: Spring flowers found in woods and along trails are often in pastel colors or white and the plants are low to the ground. Golden Ragwort stands out because it is a warm golden yellow and is usually at least 12" high when it blooms. It often grows along the sides of trails that run along streams or beneath wet cliffs or at the bottom of drainage areas.

Early Goldenrod

EARLY GOLDENROD
Solidago juncea
Composite Family (Compositae)

Description: The almost entire leaves have small, winglike leaflets at their axil and alternate on the stem of this 1–3' plant. The leaves and stem are smooth. The ¼–½" flowers are yellow and form an elm-branched cluster.

Bloom Season: July–September

Habitat/Range: In dry, open places from Nova Scotia to Saskatchewan and south to Georgia and Missouri.

Comments: The flowers of goldenrods found in the Southern Appalachian Mountains can be in the axil of the leaves, like the Blue-Stemmed Goldenrod *(Solidago caesia),* or form clusters in 1 of 3 basic shapes. The flowers can form a clublike cluster as seen in Skunk Goldenrod *(Solidago glomerata),* or they can have elm-branching clusters as does Elm-Leaved Goldenrod *(Solidago ulmifolia),* or clusters that form a group that is flat across the top as the Slender-Leaved or Slender Fragrant Goldenrod *(Solidago tenuifolia).*

SHOWY GOLDENROD
Solidago speciosa
Composite Family (Compositae)

Description: The lanceolate, toothed leaves alternate on the stem of this 2–6' plant. The stem is red. The ¼" flowers have 5–8 yellow rays (petals). The flowers form a clublike cluster.

Bloom Season: August–October

Habitat/Range: Rich fields and woodlands from New Hampshire to Minnesota and south to Georgia and Texas.

Comments: Another clublike cluster goldenrod found in the Southern Appalachian Mountains is Stout Goldenrod *(Solidago squarossa).* It can be recognized by its many large, long-stalked, toothed, elliptical leaves. Goldenrods hybridize and trained field botanists often find it hard to distinguish one species from another.

Showy Goldenrod

COLTSFOOT
Tussilago farfara
Composite Family (Compositae)

Description: The lobed leaves have the shape of a colt's foot but are absent when this 6–18" plant blooms. The 1–2" flowers have many yellow, squared petals. The seed ball is not as feathery as a dandelion seed ball.

Bloom Season: March–May

Habitat/Range: In moist soils on banks and roadsides from Nova Scotia to southwestern Virginia and Tennessee.

Comments: In the Southern Appalachian Mountains, where it can be found in the Jefferson National Forest and Hungry Mother State Park in Virginia and at low altitudes in Great Smoky Mountains National Park, this plant often blooms for more than a month and grows in large patches. It is not uncommon to see the leaves, the flower, and the seed ball in one group of plants. In the rest of the Appalachian Mountain range it is rare to see any leaves on the plant before the flowers and seeds have completely disappeared.

Coltsfoot

Coltsfoot leaves

Wingstem

WINGSTEM
Verbesina alternifolia
Composite Family (Compositae)

Description: The toothed leaves alternate on the stem of this 3–8' plant. The 1–2" yellow flowers have 10 or fewer petals and a yellow disk.

Bloom Season: August–September

Habitat/Range: In rich soils from New Jersey to Iowa and south to Kansas and Florida.

Comments: Large stands of Wingstem can be found in many locations in the Southern Appalachian Mountains—along the roadsides of Hungry Mother State Park and the Jefferson National Forest in Virginia, and along the Blue Ridge Parkway from Virginia to the Great Smoky Mountains National Park entrance in North Carolina and in the park itself.

Crown Beard

CROWN BEARD
Verbesina occidentalis
Composite Family (Compositae)

Description: The toothed, lanceolate leaves are opposite each other on the stem of this 3–6' plant. The 1–2" flowers have tufts of 1–5 yellow petals.

Bloom Season: August–October

Habitat/Range: In dry woodlands on hillsides and beside roads from Maryland to Illinois and south to Florida.

Comments: Crown Beards are sometimes called Wingstems in the Southern Appalachian Mountains. Most field guides distinguish Crown Beard with its opposite leaves from its close relative Wingstem *(Verbesina alternifolia)*, which as its botanical name indicates, has alternating leaves. Crown Beards are very common along the Blue Ridge Parkway from Virginia to North Carolina. There is a large stand of Crown Beard next to the visitors center at Peaks of Otter on the Blue Ridge Parkway in Virginia.

SPICEBUSH
Lindera benzoin
Heath Family (Ericaceae)

Description: There are no leaves on this 3–15' shrub when it flowers. The ¼" fragrant, yellow flowers form small tufts along the bare branch. When the flowers die, the leaves that emerge are ovate and alternate on the branch of the shrub.

Bloom Season: March–May

Habitat/Range: In moist, wooded areas and thickets and along streams from Maine and New Hampshire to Michigan and south to North Carolina and Kansas.

Comments: This is one of the first bushes to bloom in the spring. In the Appalachian Mountains it is often found on trails and roadsides that run along streams. There is a spicy aroma in woods where there are many Spicebush in bloom. In Great Smoky Mountains National Park, it grows mostly at low altitudes.

Spicebush

Partridge Pea

PARTRIDGE PEA
Cassia fasciculata
Pea Family (Fabaceae)

Description: The fernlike leaves alternate on the stem of this 1–2' plant. The 1–1½" flowers bloom on the axil of the leaves and have 5 yellow petals, often with bright red blotches at the center edge of the petals.

Bloom Season: July–September

Habitat/Range: In fields and along roadsides from Southern Ontario to Minnesota and south to Florida and Texas.

Comments: The stamen of Partridge Pea is very prominent and 2 or more are reddish purple. A similar plant, Wild Sensitive Plant *(Cassia nictitans),* grows in the Southern Appalachian Mountains and looks very much like the Partridge Pea plant. Everything about the plant is smaller and the flowers are about ¼" in size.

Common St. Johnswort

COMMON ST. JOHNSWORT
Hypericum perforatum
St. Johnswort Family (Guiterrae)

Description: The thin, ovate, entire leaves are opposite each other on the stem of this 12–24" multi-branched plant. The ½" flowers have 5 yellow petals with small black dots at the edge. The stamens are united in groups of 3 and raised in a prominent center grouping.

Bloom Season: June–September

Habitat/Range: A common plant of fields and waste places, found throughout the United States. A native of Europe.

Comments: The plant is used commercially to produce over-the-counter medications for controlling depression. The leaves each have glands that look like small translucent dots. These dots contain a pigment that the plant uses for photosynthesis.

WITCH HAZEL
Hamamelis virginia
Witch Hazel Family (Hamamelidaceae)

Witch Hazel

Description: The wavy-toothed, ovate leaves of this 5–15' shrub or small tree have mostly turned their autumn yellow at flowering time. The 1" flowers have 4 narrow yellow petals.

Bloom Season: September–October in most areas, and December–February in the semi-tropical climates of Florida and Texas.

Habitat/Range: In wooded areas from Nova Scotia to Ontario and south to Florida and Texas.

Comments: While hiking in the woods in October, the walker who takes the time to look closely at small trees with broad ovate leaves turning from green to yellow might be surprised to find that the branches of the tree have many bright yellow flowers. Witch hazel, an astringent, is made from this plant.

Yellow Iris

YELLOW IRIS
Iris pseudacorus
Iris Family (Iridaceae)

Description: The grasslike, 1–2" wide leaves alternate on the stem of this 1–3' plant. The 4" flowers have 3 yellow petals.

Bloom Season: April–August

Habitat/Range: In wet places by lakes and streams and in marshes from Massachusetts to southern New Jersey and at low elevations in the Great Smoky Mountains of Tennessee and North Carolina.

Comments: Yellow Iris escaped from cultivation and is found throughout the Appalachian Mountains. It is found in Great Smoky Mountains National Park at low elevations beside streams. It is also called Yellow Flag or Water Flag.

Horse Balm or Stoneroot

HORSE BALM OR STONEROOT
Collinsonia canadensis
Mint Family (Labiatae)

Description: The toothed, ovate leaves are opposite each other on the stem of this 1–3' plant. The ½", yellow, strawlike flowers have a fringed lip. The stamens and pistils are long and project far beyond the petals of the flowers.

Bloom Season: August–September

Habitat/Range: In damp, wooded areas from New Hampshire to Wisconsin and south to Florida and Arkansas.

Comments: These lemon-scented flowers form a pyramid, with just a few blooming at a time. Horse Balm is an easily overlooked, late summer woodland plant and the beauty of its delicate flowers are best appreciated when viewed through a magnifying glass.

YELLOW CLINTONIA OR CORN-LILY
Clintonia borealis
Lily Family (Lilliaceae)

Description: The large, shiny, entire leaves are at the base of this 6–12" plant. The ¾" greenish yellow, 6-petal flowers are bell shaped. The berries are blue.

Bloom Season: April–June

Habitat/Range: In moist rocky woods and high meadows from Labrador to Manitoba and south to New England, Wisconsin, and in the mountains to Georgia.

Comments: Yellow Clintonia, sometimes called Bluebead Lily, is normally found only in northern climates, but grows at the higher elevations in the Southern Appalachian Mountains. Another clintonia with smaller white flowers *(Clintonia umbellata)* and similar leaves can be found on the Roaring Fork Nature Motor Trail in Great Smoky Mountains National Park. It has black berries.

Yellow Clintonia or Corn-Lily

Yellow Mandarin or Fairy Bells

VICTOR MEDINA

YELLOW MANDARIN OR FAIRY BELLS
Disporum lanuginosum
Lily Family (Lilliaceae)

Description: The wavy-edged, ovate leaves alternate on the stem of this 1–2' plant. The 1" flowers have 6 yellow-greenish petals and are bell shaped. 1 or 2 flowers hang from almost horizontal branches.

Bloom Season: April–June

Habitat/Range: In wooded areas, mostly in the Appalachian Mountains.

Comments: Fairy Bells are relatively common in the Southern Appalachian Mountains and rarely found anywhere else. By mid-April, Fairy Bells bloom in Great Smoky Mountains National Park along the Chimney Top Nature Trail and in Georgia along the nature trail of Fort Mountain State Park and the Sosebee Cove area of Chattahoochee National Forest.

Yellow Adder's Tongue or Yellow Trout Lily

YELLOW ADDER'S TONGUE OR YELLOW TROUT LILY

Erythronium americanum
Lily Family (Lilliaceae)

Description: The 4–8" entire, lanceolate leaves are at the base of this 3–6" plant. The leaves are smooth and have a mottled appearance when they first appear. The 1–2" flowers have 6 yellow, bell-shaped, and reflexed petals and bright red stamens.

Bloom Season: March–May

Habitat/Range: In moist rich woods and thickets from Nova Scotia to Minnesota and south to Florida.

Comments: This plant can be found throughout the Appalachian range. The Iroquois used the roots to control fevers, and the leaves were used to heal skin ulcers. This plant is also called Dog Tooth Violet. Trout Lily often grows in large groups on stream banks and in moist gullies like that found in Georgia's Chattahoochee National Forest at Sosebee Cove.

YELLOW DAY LILY OR LEMON DAY LILY
Hemerocallis flava
Lily Family (Lilliaceae)

Description: The 2'-long, broad, lanceolate leaves are at the base of this 2–5' plant. The 3–4" flowers have 6 yellow petals and are funnel shaped.

Bloom Season: June

Habitat/Range: In open areas near gardens and previously inhabited areas in regions with extensive plant diversity such as the Southern Appalachian Mountains.

Comments: The Orange Day Lily *(Hemerocallis fulva)* is much more commonly found in forests and parks. Both plants are natives of Asia. The Yellow Day Lily can be found in the Cades Cove area of Great Smoky Mountains National Park.

Yellow Day Lily or Lemon Day Lily

Yellow Trillium or Yellow Toadshade

YELLOW TRILLIUM OR YELLOW TOADSHADE
Trillium luteum
Lily Family (Lilliaceae)

Description: The large, spotted, ovate leaves form a whorl of 3 on the stem of this 6–12" plant. The 2–3", yellow, cup-shaped flowers have 3 petals.

Bloom Season: April–May

Habitat/Range: On wooded hillsides and along roadsides in the southern United States.

Comments: In Great Smoky Mountains National Park in April, there are several sites where many Yellow Trillium grow. The hillside abutting Chimney Top Picnic Grove has a great variety of flowers, but the Fringed Phacelia *(Phacelia fimbriata)* and the Yellow Trillium dominate. Yellow Trillium can also be spotted along River Road and on the Roaring Forks Motor Nature Trail.

Perfoliate Bellwort

PERFOLIATE BELLWORT
Uvularia perfoliata
Lily Family (Lilliaceae)

Description: The ovate, entire leaves alternate on the stem of this 6–18" plant. The stem pierces the leaves. The 1–1½", pale yellow, 6-petal flowers are bell shaped.

Bloom Season: April–June

Habitat/Range: In moist woods from Quebec and Ontario south to Florida and Mississippi.

Comments: Perfoliate Bellwort is found in mid-April along the red blaze trail in Fort Deposit State Park, Alabama, and along the nature trail in Fort Mountain State Park, Georgia. Large-Flowered Bellwort *(Uvularia grandiflora)* also grows in the Southern Appalachian Mountains but has a brighter yellow, large flower, the stem does not pierce the leaves, and its 6 petals hang down close to each other.

SESSILE BELLWORT OR WILD OATS
Uvularia sessilifolia
Lily Family (Lilliaceae)

Description: The lanceolate, smooth leaves alternate on the stem of this 6–10" plant. The ½–¾", bell-shaped flowers have 6 pale yellow petals.

Bloom Season: April–June

Habitat/Range: Common in woods and thickets from New Brunswick to Minnesota and south to Georgia and Arkansas.

Comments: The plant can be found in the Cades Cove area of Great Smoky Mountains National Park and in the Bear Creek recreation area of the Jefferson National Forest in Virginia. In the 18th century, the young shoots of this plant were considered a delicacy, tasting like asparagus. However tempting it is to revive this practice, remember that plants in state or national parks and forests cannot be disturbed and we have so few woodlands today that if the plants were harvested in the wild they would become extinct.

Sessile Bellwort or Wild Oats

SEEDBOX
Ludwigia alternifolia
Evening Primrose Family (Onagraceae)

Description: The entire, lanceolate leaves alternate on the stem of this 1–3' plant. The ½–1" flowers have 4 yellow petals and grow on short stalks in the axil of the leaves.

Bloom Season: July–September

Habitat/Range: In swamps and along streams and lakes from Ontario to Iowa and south to Florida and Texas.

Comments: Seedbox is also called Rattle-Box because the seed capsule is square on the top. It was named after C. G. Ludwig, a botanist in the early 18th century. It can be found in Great Smoky Mountains National Park at low elevations.

Seedbox

Common Evening Primrose

COMMON EVENING PRIMROSE
Oenothera biennis
Evening Primrose Family (Onagraceae)

Description: The lanceolate, slightly toothed leaves alternate on the stem of this 2–6' plant. The 1½–2" flowers have 4 yellow, notched petals that are usually closed during the day.

Bloom Season: May–October

Habitat/Range: In dry soils from Nova Scotia to Alberta and south to North Carolina and Texas.

Comments: This is another genus of plants that hybridize. There are about 15 species of *Oenothera* that grow in the eastern United States. One group, Evening Primrose, opens its petals as the sun starts to set, and the other group (known as Sundrops) has open flowers in sunshine. The common type of Sundrop found in the Southern Appalachian Mountains is *Oenothera fruticosa*. All of the *Oenothera* have 4 branched stigma that form a cross, and most have notched, yellow petals.

Yellow Lady's Slipper

YELLOW LADY'S SLIPPER
Cypripedium calceolus
Orchid Family (Orchidaceae)

Description: The elongated, ovate leaves alternate on the stem of this 8–12" plant. The 1–2" yellow flowers have an open pouch. The lateral petals are usually twisted.

Bloom Season: April–July

Habitat/Range: In bogs, swamps, and woodlands from Newfoundland to British Columbia and Washington and south to New Jersey, the mountains of Georgia and Tennessee, Missouri, Texas, and New Mexico.

Comments: There are several Lady's Slippers, and the yellow one's home is usually mountains and northern climates. Yellow Lady's Slippers are less commonly found in the Appalachian Mountains than Pink Lady's Slippers *(Cypripedium acaule)*. Yellow Lady's Slippers are smaller than Pink Lady's Slipper, and their botanical name means Aphrodite's slipper. It grows in both Great Smoky Mountains National Park in Tennessee and North Carolina and in Fort Mountain State Park in Georgia.

SQUAWROOT
Conopholis americana
Broomrape Family (Orobanchaceae)

Description: This 4–8" parasitic plant has no leaves. The ½" flowers are yellowish and grow beneath the brownish scales. The plant resembles an upright pinecone.

Bloom Season: April–June

Habitat/Range: At the base of trees in rich, wooded areas from Maine to Ontario and south to Florida and Michigan.

Comments: Squawroot is a parasite on tree roots, particularly oak trees. During times of drought, fewer plants come up in the affected woodland. It can be found in April in Great Smoky Mountains National Park on the Chimney Top Nature Trail and on woodland trails just off the Blue Ridge Parkway in North Carolina.

Squawroot

Yellow Wood Sorrel

YELLOW WOOD SORREL
Oxalis stricta
Wood Sorrel Family (Oxalidaceae)

Description: The 3 leaves have 3 rounded leaflets that bend in half at dusk and flatten when the sun shines. The leaves alternate on the stem of this 3–8" plant. The ¼–½" flowers have 5 yellow petals.

Bloom Season: May–September

Habitat/Range: In wooded areas and fields from Nova Scotia to Wyoming and Colorado and south to Florida.

Comments: Another small yellow wood sorrel *(Oxalis europaea)* grows in the Appalachian Mountains. It can easily be distinguished from the wood sorrel shown only when the seed pods appear, since only the seed pods of *Oxalis stricta* are bent downward from the stem.

Celandine

CELANDINE
Chelidonium majus
Poppy Family (Papaveraceae)

Description: The leaves, divided into lobed leaflets, alternate on the stem of this 1–2' plant. The ¾–1" flowers have 4 yellow petals.

Bloom Season: May–June

Habitat/Range: In moist soils from Maine to Pennsylvania and in North Carolina.

Comments: Celandines are native to Europe and were once used medicinally. Queen Elizabeth I reportedly removed a rotten tooth with an application of the powdered root. The plants are usually found at the edge of woods and near streams.

CELANDINE POPPY
Stylophorum diphyllum
Poppy Family (Papaveraceae)

Description: The many-toothed and deeply lobed leaves are opposite each other on the stem of this 1–1½' plant. The 1½–2" flowers have 4 large, yellow petals.

Bloom Season: March–June

Habitat/Range: In damp, wooded areas from western Pennsylvania mountains to Wisconsin and south. Also on the Piedmont and Coastal Plain from Maryland south to Virginia, Tennessee, and Missouri.

Comments: The seed pod of Celandine Poppy is hairy and silver colored. The undersides of the leaves also have this silvery sheen. The juice of the plant is bright yellow. It is common to find one solitary plant in a location.

Celandine Poppy

MONEYWORT OR CREEPING LOOSESTRIFE

Lysimachia nummularia
Primrose Family (Primulaceae)

Description: The almost round, entire leaves are opposite each other on the stem of this creeping plant. The 1" flowers have 5 bright yellow petals and grow in the axil of the leaves.

Bloom Season: June–August

Habitat/Range: In moist places and lawns from Newfoundland to Michigan and south to Georgia and Kansas.

Comments: Moneywort is a European plant that is now naturalized in lawns and wet places throughout the northeastern and north-central parts of North America. It can be found in open areas at low altitudes throughout the Southern Appalachian Mountains.

Moneywort or Creeping Loosestrife

Yellow Whorled Loosestrife

YELLOW WHORLED LOOSESTRIFE

Lysimachia quadrifolia
Primrose Family (Primulaceae)

Description: The tapering, lanceolate leaves form whorls of 4 or 5 on the stem of this 10–18" plant. The ¾–1" yellow flowers have 5 petals and grow on long stalks.

Bloom Season: July–August

Habitat/Range: In thickets and open, wooded areas from New Brunswick to Ontario and south to Tennessee and Georgia.

Comments: This is one of several yellow loosestrifes found in the Appalachian Mountains. Yellow Loosestrife, or Swamp Candles *(Lythrum terrestris),* a plant of marshes and other wet places, has a terminal spike of bright yellow, 5-petal flowers and grows in both the Southern and Northern Appalachian Mountains.

Kidneyleaf Buttercup or Small-Flowered Crowfoot

KIDNEYLEAF BUTTERCUP OR SMALL-FLOWERED CROWFOOT
Ranunculus abortivus
Buttercup Family (Ranunculaceae)

Description: A kidney-shaped leaf grows from the base of this 6–18" plant. The stem leaves are toothed and lobed and alternate on the stem. The ¼" flowers have very small yellow petals.

Bloom Season: April–June

Habitat/Range: In wooded areas and moist grounds from Labrador and Nova Scotia south to Florida.

Comments: Although the flower is very small, the plant is often noticed because it is among the earliest fairly tall plants to bloom in the woods.

HISPID BUTTERCUP OR HAIRY BUTTERCUP
Ranunculus hispidus
Buttercup Family (Ranunculaceae)

Description: The leaves, divided into 3 toothed segments, alternate on the stem of this 1–2' plant. The 5 small petals are yellow and longer than they are wide.

Bloom Season: March–June

Habitat/Range: In dry, wooded areas and meadows from Vermont and Ontario to North Dakota and south to Georgia and Arkansas.

Comments: The genus of all buttercups is *Ranunculus*, which means "little frog." Most buttercups are found in wet places—some with their roots completely under water, others on wet banks and bogs, and others still in areas that are periodically moist. *R. hispidus* is one of the few that can flourish in both dry woods and woods that very occasionally flood.

Hispid Buttercup or Hairy Buttercup

Creeping Buttercup

CREEPING BUTTERCUP
Ranunculus repens
Buttercup Family (Ranunculaceae)

Description: The divided, dark green leaves alternate on the stem of this 6–18" plant. The 1" flowers have 5 yellow petals.

Bloom Season: April–May

Habitat/Range: Roadsides and meadows in wet grounds from Newfoundland to Georgia. Also found in British Columbia.

Comments: This buttercup likes to have its feet wet and grows on wet ground beside a small stream in the Cades Cove area of Great Smoky National Park and in a wet area of Sosebee Cove in the Chattachoochee National Forest in Georgia.

Agrimony

AGRIMONY
Agrimonia gryposepala
Rose Family (Rosaceae)

Description: The divided leaves are the most distinctive characteristic of this 4–8" plant. The leaflets are toothed ovals. The large leaflets diminish in size toward the end, and large and very small leaflets alternate. Several small, yellow flowers, each with 5 symmetric petals, climb a slender spike. The stems are downy.

Bloom Season: June–September

Habitat/Range: The plant is found at the edges of woods and thickets from Quebec to North Dakota and south to Georgia and Kansas.

Comments: Agrimony or agrimonia is an old Greek name for a wound in the eye, which this plant was supposed to cure. The small burs of this plant stick to clothes. Agrimony can be found growing in the Cascade and Mount Rogers Recreation Areas of Jefferson National Forest in Virginia.

INDIAN STRAWBERRY
Dushesnea indica
Rose Family (Rosaceae)

Description: The leaves have 3 toothed leaflets and are at the base of this creeping plant. The ½–¾" flowers have 5 yellow petals and 5 green bracts visible below the petals.

Bloom Season: April–June

Habitat/Range: In open, wooded areas and fields from New York to Iowa south to Florida.

Comments: The fruit looks like a wild strawberry, but it is tasteless. Indian Strawberry blooms by April on the Visitor Center Nature Trail and the Roaring Forks Motor Nature Trail in Great Smoky Mountains National Park.

Indian Strawberry

YELLOW AVENS
Geum aleppicum
Rose Family (Rosaceae)

Yellow Avens

Description: The divided and toothed leaves alternate on the stem of this 2–4' plant, and each lower set of leaflets is usually smaller than the one above. The 1" flowers have 5 yellow petals and a bristly center disk.

Bloom Season: May–August

Habitat/Range: In meadows, thickets, and wooded areas from Nova Scotia south to Pennsylvania, and at high elevations in the Southern Appalachian Mountains.

Comments: This is another example of a plant that is normally only found in northern climates that also grows in the Southern Appalachian Mountains. The species name of the plant, *aleppicum,* comes from the name of a town in Syria.

Dwarf Cinquefoil

DWARF CINQUEFOIL
Potentilla canadensis
Rose Family (Rosaceae)

Description: The leaves, at the base of this spreading, low plant, have 5 leaflets with teeth only on their upper half. The ¼–½" yellow flowers have 5 petals.

Bloom Season: April–June

Habitat/Range: In poor soil from Maine to Ontario and south to Georgia and Ohio. Often found along trails and roadsides.

Comments: At first glance Dwarf Cinquefoil *(Potentilla canadensis)* and Common Cinquefoil *(Potentilla simplex)* look very much alike. The only difference between the plants is in the leaflets, which on Common Cinquefoil have teeth from top to bottom. The name cinquefoil in both plants refers to the fact that the leaves have 5 leaflets.

Yellow Corydalis

YELLOW CORYDALIS
Corydalis flavula
Snapdragon Family (Scrophulariaceae)

Description: The finely cut leaves alternate on the stem of this 6–16" plant. The ½" yellow flowers have a spur, and the top petal has small teeth.

Bloom Season: April–June

Habitat/Range: In rocky woods from New York to Southern Ontario and south to North Carolina and Louisiana.

Comments: The roots of most of the *Corydalis* species are potentially toxic. A close look helps to tell one corydalis from another as the flowers are small but have distinctive differences which can easily be seen with a hand-held magnifier. The small teeth on the top petal of this corydalis distinguish it from other similar plants.

SMOOTH FALSE FOXGLOVE
Gerardia flava
Snapdragon Family (Scrophulariaceae)

Description: The upper leaves are lanceolate and the lower ones are deeply lobed. Both types of leaves are opposite on the stem of this 2–6' plant. The stem has a purplish hue. The 1–2", bell-shaped flowers have 5 light yellow petals.

Bloom Season: July–September

Habitat/Range: In open sunny places from southern Maine to Georgia and west to Wisconsin.

Comments: The plant is a parasite on oak tree roots. It can be found in Virginia on the Sharp Mountain Trail off the Blue Ridge Parkway near Peaks of Otter, on the Appalachian Trail near where it crosses Route 311 in Jefferson National Forest, and in Hungry Mother State Park.

Smooth False Foxglove

Butter and Eggs

BUTTER AND EGGS
Linaria vulgaris
Snapdragon Family (Scrophulariaceae)

Description: The grasslike leaves alternate on the stem of this 6–18" plant. The ¾–1" snapdragon-shaped flowers are yellow and orange and grow in spikes.

Bloom Season: May–October

Habitat/Range: On roadsides and in fields almost everywhere in North America.

Comments: Also called Common Toadflax because it came from Europe, where it is a common weed among the flax plants. Other common names such as Bread & Cheese refer to the yellow flower with an orange inset. Although not usually a problem on land that is not cultivated, it can be a troublesome weed in gardens as it spreads from an underground root, and once established it is difficult to eliminate.

Common Mullein

COMMON MULLEIN
Verbascum thapsus
Snapdragon Family (Scrophulariaceae)

Description: The large, soft, velvety leaves alternate on the stem of this 4–10' plant. The ½–¾", 5-petal, yellow flowers bloom a few at a time on a long stalk at the top of the plant.

Bloom Season: June–September

Habitat/Range: In waste places and fields from Nova Scotia to South Dakota and south to Florida. Also in California and Kansas.

Comments: A native of Europe, it is naturalized in most areas in the United States and is a pesky weed in some areas. In Europe there are many myths associated with the tall wand of the plant. One myth was that it had the power to ward off evil and was called Aaron's Rod. The seeds are a narcotic to fish.

VIRGINIA GROUND-CHERRY
Physalis virginiana
Potato Family (Solanaceae)

Description: The ovate leaves alternate on the downy stem of this 1–3' plant. The 1½–2" flowers have 5 greenish yellow, shallowly cut lobes and are bell shaped.

Bloom Season: April–July

Habitat/Range: In fields, clearings, and open, wooded areas from New England to Manitoba south to South Carolina, Alabama, and Arkansas.

Comments: Virginia Ground-Cherry can be found at low altitudes in Great Smoky Mountains National Park. The pods look like miniature Japanese lanterns.

Virginia Ground-Cherry

YELLOW PIMPERNEL
Taenidia integerrima
Parsley Family (Umbelliferae)

Description: The leaves, divided into 3 top and 2 lower opposite, ovate leaflets, alternate on the stem of this 1–3' plant. Each tiny yellow flower has 5 petals. The flowers form a flat umbel.

Bloom Season: May–June

Habitat/Range: In meadows, dry, open woodlands, and on rocky hillsides from Quebec to North Carolina. Also found in several Midwest states and Mississippi.

Comments: The botanical name refers to the narrow ribs on the fruit. Yellow Pimpernel can be found at low and middle altitudes of Great Smoky Mountains National Park.

Yellow Pimpernel

Golden Alexander

GOLDEN ALEXANDER
Zizia aurea
Parsley Family (Umbelliferae)

Description: The 2–3 times divided leaves alternate on the stem of this 1–2' plant. The leaflets are ovate with fine teeth. The tiny flowers are yellow and form an umbel. Each flower has 5 petals.

Bloom Season: April–June

Habitat/Range: Along trails, in open, wooded areas, and in meadows from New Brunswick to Saskatchewan and south to Florida, South Dakota, and Texas.

Comments: Golden Alexander blooms in April in Virginia at Hungry Mother State Park and Cascade Recreation Area in Jefferson National Forest and at Chestnut Hill in Great Smoky Mountains National Park. Blooms later in the mountains of northern Virginia.

Halberd-Leaved Yellow Violet

HALBERD-LEAVED YELLOW VIOLET
Viola hastata
Violet Family (Violacaea)

Description: The elongated, heart-shaped leaves alternate on the stem of this 3–6" plant. The ½" flowers have 5 yellow petals with purple lines at the throat of the flower. The flowers grow on the same stem as the leaves.

Bloom Season: March–May

Habitat/Range: In moist, mountainous or hilly, wooded areas from Pennsylvania to Ohio and south to Florida.

Comments: This yellow violet grows in the Appalachian Mountains from the western part of Pennsylvania south. It can be found in the Great Smoky Mountains National Park, in Alabama at Fort Desoto State Park on the Red Blaze Trail, and in Georgia at Fort Mountain State Park on the nature trail and Sosebee Cove area of Chattahoochee National Forest.

SMOOTH YELLOW VIOLET
Viola pensylvanica
Violet Family (Violacaea)

Description: The heart-shaped, toothed, smooth leaves alternate on the stem of this 4–12" plant. The ½–¾" flowers have 5 yellow petals.

Bloom Season: March–June

Habitat/Range: In moist, wooded areas from Maine to Georgia.

Comments: This is a very common yellow violet found throughout the eastern United States. It commonly grows in large groups, often near the base of trees. Smooth Yellow Violet produces a prominent, fuzzy, white seed pod.

Smooth Yellow Violet

ORANGE FLOWERS

VICTOR MEDINA

Orange Jewelweed

Butterfly Weed or Pleurisy Root

BUTTERFLY WEED OR PLEURISY ROOT

Asclepias tuberosa
Milkweed Family (Asclepiadaceae)

Description: The lanceolate, entire leaves alternate on the stem of this 1–2' plant. The ¼–½" flowers are orange and yellow or just orange and form a flat umbel. Each flower has 5 petals, and each petal has a pointed crown and dangling points.

Bloom Season: June–September

Habitat/Range: From Maine to Minnesota and south to Florida and Texas.

Comments: At first glance, this eye-catching plant might not look like a milkweed. It is one of the few milkweeds whose leaves alternate on the stem of the plant and whose flowers do not form a round cluster. But the bright flowers do have the typical milkweed flower shape.

ORANGE JEWELWEED OR SPOTTED TOUCH-ME-NOT
Impatiens capensis
Jewelweed Family (Balsaminaceae)

Description: The slightly toothed, broad, ovate leaves alternate on the stem of this 2–5' plant. The 1" orange flowers form a tilted cup with a lip. The flower has brown spots at the bottom of the cup.

Bloom Season: June–September

Habitat/Range: In damp wooded areas from Newfoundland to Saskatchewan and south to South Carolina, Alabama, and Oklahoma.

Comments: English settlers brought over many of the area's wild plants, which then became naturalized. Orange Jewelweed, a North American native, has been naturalized in England where it is called American Jewelweed. The plant is called Touch-Me-Not because when the seed pods dry they explode at the lightest touch.

VICTOR MEDINA

Orange Jewelweed or Spotted Touch-Me-Not

Trumpet Creeper

TRUMPET CREEPER
Campsis radicans
Bignonia Family (Bignoniaceae)

Description: The ovate, toothed leaflets are opposite each other on the stem of this vine. The 2–3", trumpet-shaped flowers have 5 red or orange petals. The stem is woody.

Bloom Season: June–September

Habitat/Range: At the edge of moist woods, in thickets, or on roadsides from New Jersey to Iowa and in the southeastern United States.

Comments: The vine lacks tendrils but climbs by means of aerial roots. The bright flowers can often be seen along roadsides.

Flame Azalea

FLAME AZALEA
Rhododendron calendulaceum
Heath Family (Ericaceae)

Description: The leaves on this 2–15' shrub are ovate and entire. The 2–3", tubed flowers are usually orange but can have a range of hues toward the red. The 5 petals are flared and the 5 stamens protrude beyond the petals.

Bloom Season: April–June

Habitat/Range: Dry woodlands from southwestern Pennsylvania to southeastern Ohio and south to Georgia.

Comments: The plant is native to dry North American woodlands but has been cultivated extensively. In the Appalachian Mountains it is most commonly found in the western part of the range from southern Pennsylvania south to Georgia. Flame Azalea can be found in Great Smoky Mountains National Park.

Orange Day Lily

ORANGE DAY LILY
Hemerocallis fulva
Lily Family (Lilliaceae)

Description: The 2', lanceolate leaves are at the base of this 2–3' plant. The 3–5" flowers have 6 orange petals and are funnel shaped. The stem forks repeatedly, and there is a bud on each stem.

Bloom Season: May–July

Habitat/Range: A hybrid of day lilies from Asia, this plant has escaped from cultivation and is common in the eastern United States.

Comments: Orange Day Lily grows throughout the Appalachian Mountains. Each flower opens in the morning and lasts for one day. The buds of the flowers are used in Chinese cooking and produce the same results as cooking with okra, thickening the cooking liquid.

Carolina Lily

CAROLINA LILY
Lilium michauxii
Lily Family (Lilliaceae)

Description: The lanceolate leaves are opposite each other on the stem of this 1–3' plant. The middle leaves are wider than those at either end of the stem. The 3" flowers have 6 recurved, orange petals.

Bloom Season: July–September

Habitat/Range: In meadows, on high mountain balds, and at the edges of wooded roadsides from Virginia south to Florida.

Comments: Carolina Lily can be found along the Blue Ridge Parkway. The plant is usually 3' or less with 4 or fewer flowers on each plant.

TURK'S CAP LILY
Lilium superbum
Lily Family (Lilliaceae)

Description: The lanceolate leaves form whorls on the stem of this 3–8' plant. The leaves are smooth. The 4" flowers have 6 flexed petals that are orange with brown dots and a center with green edges.

Bloom Season: June–August

Habitat/Range: In swamps, along streams, and in fields from Ontario to Minnesota and south to Georgia, Alabama, and Nebraska.

Comments: Turk's Cap Lily plants tend to be very tall with many flowers whose petals and sepals turn sharply back on themselves, blooming on the plant at once. The shape of the flower resembles the hats worn by ancient Turks. The plant often blooms in July along Newfoundland Gap Road in Great Smoky Mountains National Park.

Turk's Cap Lily

PINK AND PURPLE FLOWERS

Gray Beardtongue

Wild Petunia

WILD PETUNIA
Ruellia humilis
Acanthus Family (Acanthaceae)

Description: The stalkless, lanceolate leaves are opposite each other on the stem of this 1–2" plant. The 1–2" flowers have 5 pink or purple connected petals.

Bloom Season: June–August

Habitat/Range: In dry, wooded areas and clearings from New Jersey to Illinois and south to Florida and Texas.

Comments: Several varieties of wild petunia grow in the southern Appalachian Mountains. *Ruellia caroliniens* is probably the most common, and it looks very much like the pictured plant, but the leaves are more downy. It is sometimes difficult to determine which one of the wild petunias is blooming because the plants hybridize. The plant is cultivated, and sometimes commercial nurseries refer to it as *Ruellia.*

SWAMP MILKWEED
Asclepias incarnata
Milkweed Family (Asclepiadaceae)

Description: The lanceolate leaves are opposite each other on the stem of this 1–3' plant. The ¼", 5-petal flowers are pink and white and form a flat cluster.

Bloom Season: July–September

Habitat/Range: In swamps and at the edges of ponds and lakes from New Brunswick to Saskatchewan and south to Colorado and Tennessee.

Comments: Look closely and it becomes apparent that each flower of this beautiful plant does have the distinctive shape of milkweed flowers—the 5 petals that seem to flare up and 5 petals that point down. The plant grows at low elevations in Great Smoky Mountains National Park.

Swamp Milkweed

Common Milkweed

COMMON MILKWEED
Asclepias syriaca
Milkweed Family (Asclepiadaceae)

Description: The short-stalked, oblong leaves are opposite each other on the stem of this 1–3' plant. The leaves are downy beneath. The ¼" flowers are purplish or pink, and each has 5 petals, each with a pointed crown and dangling points. The flowers form round, somewhat drooping heads.

Bloom Season: June–July

Habitat/Range: In fields and meadows from New Brunswick to Saskatchewan and south to North Carolina and Kansas.

Comments: During World War II, milkweeds were harvested for the floss on their seeds to produce life jackets and flight suits. The floss was found to be much more buoyant than cork and warmer, with a weight equal to wool.

Virginia Bluebell or Virginia Cowslip

VIRGINIA BLUEBELL OR VIRGINIA COWSLIP
Mertensia virginica
Borage Family (Boraginaceae)

Description: The large, ovate, entire leaves alternate on the stem of this 1–2' plant. The 1", 5-petal, trumpet-shaped flowers are pink at first and turn blue as they develop.

Bloom Season: March–May

Habitat/Range: In rich woods, meadows, and on the floodplains of rivers and streams from New York to Minnesota and south to South Carolina, Alabama, Arkansas, and Kansas.

Comments: Occasionally in a sea of blue Virginia Bluebells, a few pure white plants will grow. Virginia Bluebells are often found in large colonies near those rivers and streams that often overflow their banks.

PURPLE CRESS
Cardamine douglassii
Mustard Family (Brassicaceae)

Description: The toothed and lanceolate stem leaves alternate on the stem, and toothed and heart-shaped leaves are at the base of this 6–12" plant. The ½–¾" flowers have 4 rose-purple petals.

Bloom Season: March–May

Habitat/Range: In moist places from western Massachusetts to Wisconsin and south to Virginia and Tennessee.

Comments: In mid-April the hill that the Appalachian Trail climbs on the north side of Route 311 in the Jefferson National Forest of Virginia is covered with Purple Cress.

Purple Cress

Cut-Leaved Toothwort or Pepperroot

CUT-LEAVED TOOTHWORT OR PEPPERROOT
Dentaria laciniata
Mustard Family (Brassicaceae)

Description: The finely divided, toothed leaves form whorls of 3 on the stem of this 6–12" plant. The ½–1", bell-shaped flowers have 4 white or pink petals.

Bloom Season: March–June

Habitat/Range: In moist or rich wooded areas from Quebec to Florida and west to Minnesota.

Comments: Cut-Leaved Toothwort is the most common of the toothworts in the Appalachian Mountains. Native Americans ate the rhizomes (roots) of this plant, which have a peppery taste. The leaves are edible, and some people prefer pepperroot leaves and roots to other greens and potatoes.

Venus's Looking Glass

VENUS'S LOOKING GLASS
Specularia perfoliata
Bluebell Family (Campanulaceae)

Description: The heart-shaped, toothed leaves alternate and clasp the stem of this 6–30" plant. The ½–1" star-shaped flowers have 5 blue or purple petals. Only the flowers in the axils of the top leaves open.

Bloom Season: May–August

Habitat/Range: In woods and fields from Maine to British Columbia and south to Florida, Texas, and Mexico.

Comments: Some field guides place Venus's Looking Glass in the lobelia family *(Lobeliodeae)* and give it the botanical name *Triodanis perfoliata.* Field guides that place the plant in the lobelia family do not necessarily place it in the *Triodanis* genus. Some of the confusion comes about because its common name and *Specularia* were derived from a Latin word meaning "mirror." Only the seed of the plant has a shiny surface, and many botanists felt that *Specularia* was a misnomer, hence the renaming of the genus.

SOUTHERN ARROWWOOD
Viburnum dentatum
Honeysuckle Family (Caprifoliaceae)

Description: The pointed, ovate leaves are opposite each other on the stem of this 3–8' shrub or small tree. The ¼" flowers have 5 pink or white petals and form a flat cluster.

Bloom Season: April–June

Habitat/Range: Along roadsides and in open, wooded areas from Pennsylvania and Tennessee south to Missouri.

Comments: From mid-April to June, many flowering shrubs and small trees bloom and add beauty to the Blue Ridge Parkway. Southern Arrowwood is one of the earliest, often blooming by early April.

Southern Arrowwood

DEPTFORD PINK
Dianthus armeria
Pink Family (Caryophyllaceae)

Deptford Pink

Description: The grasslike leaves are opposite each other on the stem of this 6–15" plant. The ½", vivid pink flowers have 5 petals with little white dots. Although the flowers are small, they are so bright that they call attention to themselves.

Bloom Season: June–September

Habitat/Range: In fields and along trails and roadsides from Quebec and southern Ontario south to Iowa and Georgia.

Comments: Deptford Pinks are one of the very few flowering plants in the grasses along the edge of woodland trails. There are no native species of *Dianthus* in the United States. Deptford Pink has found a home and is seen everywhere in the Southern Appalachian Mountains.

Bouncing Bet or Soapwort

BOUNCING BET OR SOAPWORT
Saponaria officinalis
Pink Family (Caryophyllaceae)

Description: The entire leaves are opposite each other on the stem of this 1–2' plant. The 1" flowers have 5 white or pink petals at the end of a tube.

Bloom Season: May–October

Habitat/Range: In open and waste places. The plant is native to Europe and escaped from gardens. It is found in most areas of the eastern United States.

Comments: The crushed roots and leaves make a soaplike lather. In Europe the plant is used medicinally in the form of a tea, but large doses can be poisonous.

Common Burdock

COMMON BURDOCK
Arctium minus
Composite Family (Compositae)

Description: The ovate leaves alternate on the stem of this 3–8' coarse plant. The 1–1½" purple flowers form tufts at the top of a bur.

Bloom Season: July

Habitat/Range: In waste places from Ontario to southern New York and Pennsylvania.

Comments: A plant similar in appearance, but larger in total size and with smaller flowers and leaves, Great Burdock *(Arctium lappa)*, also grows in the Southern Appalachian Mountains. Common Burdock grows around Sandstone Falls in New River Park, West Virginia.

NEW ENGLAND ASTER
Aster novae-angliae
Composite Family (Compositae)

Description: The lanceolate leaves deeply clasp the stem of this 3–6' plant. The many long, narrow, entire leaves alternate on the stem. The 1–2", showy flowers are purple or rose with a yellow disk.

Bloom Season: August–October

Habitat/Range: The plants are found in fields and along the edges of swamps and streams from Quebec to Georgia and in Colorado.

Comments: New England Aster, one of the showiest of the native asters, grows along the Blue Ridge Parkway and in the Cascade Recreation Area of Jefferson National Forest in Virginia. This species has been used to create the commercially available asters now seen in many a garden. Some Native Americans believed that smoking this plant in a pipe would attract game.

New England Aster

Purple-Stemmed Aster

PURPLE-STEMMED ASTER
Aster puniceus
Composite Family (Compositae)

Description: The toothed, clasping leaves alternate on the stem of this 2–7' plant. The 1–1½" flowers have lilac or purple rays and a yellow disk. The stem of the plant is usually reddish or purple.

Bloom Season: August–October

Habitat/Range: In swamps and wet thickets from Newfoundland to Manitoba and south to Ohio and Maryland and through the mountain states to Georgia.

Comments: Purple-Stemmed Aster grows in the Appalachian Mountains from Newfoundland to Georgia. Look for them growing along the Blue Ridge Parkway in September in Virginia and North Carolina.

Short's Aster

SHORT'S ASTER
Aster shortii
Composite Family (Compositae)

Description: The lanceolate or narrowly heart-shaped, toothed leaves alternate on the stem of this 1–4' plant. The ½–1" flowers have light purple rays and a yellow center. The stem branches, with several flowers sometimes growing at the end of each branch.

Bloom Season: August–October

Habitat/Range: In open woodlands and at the edges of wooded areas from Pennsylvania and Virginia to Iowa and Wisconsin and south to Georgia and Alabama.

Comments: Short's Aster grows in the natural islands located at the lookouts along the Blue Ridge Parkway in Virginia and North Carolina. Another purple aster found in this region is the Late Purple Aster *(Aster patens),* which has clasping, entire leaves, unlike *A. Shortii,* which has heart-shaped leaves on a long stalk.

BROWN KNAPWEED
Centaurea jacea
Composite Family (Compositae)

Description: The slightly toothed, lanceolate leaves alternate on the stem of this 1–3' plant. The small flowers have 5 rose purple petals and grow in heads about 1½" wide.

Bloom Season: June–September

Habitat/Range: Along roadsides and in fields from Quebec to Iowa and south to Tennessee and North Carolina.

Comments: A similar-looking plant, Black Knapweed *(Centaurea nigra),* also grows in the Southern Appalachian Mountains. Brown Knapweed has no fringes on its bracts, and Black Knapweed has a black edge with fringes on its bracts. Brown Knapweed can be found along the roadsides of both Hungry Mother State Park in Virginia and the Deep Creek area in Great Smoky Mountains National Park in North Carolina.

Brown Knapweed

Spotted Knapweed

SPOTTED KNAPWEED
Centaurea maculosa
Composite Family (Compositae)

Description: The divided fernlike leaves alternate on the stem of this 1–3' plant. The 1–1½" flowers form purple or pink heads.

Bloom Season: July–September

Habitat/Range: In open areas from Massachusetts to Tennessee and westward to Kentucky and Missouri.

Comments: Spotted Knapweed grows in large groups. It is a non-native plant, and in some areas it is so dense it threatens to take over the large variety of native plants that would normally be found in open places. It grows along the Blue Ridge Parkway in the Peaks of Otter area.

Tall Thistle

TALL THISTLE
Cirsium altissimum
Composite Family (Compositae)

Description: The deeply lobed, pointed leaves alternate on the stem of this 6–12' plant. The top leaves surround the flower head. The 1½–2" flowers form a pink or purple head.

Bloom Season: July–October

Habitat/Range: In wet fields and river bottoms from Massachusetts to North Dakota and south to Florida and Texas.

Comments: The distinguishing characteristic of this thistle is how tall it can grow. Specimens at the Deep Creek area of Great Smoky Mountains National Park often reach 12'.

CANADA THISTLE
Cirsium arvense
Composite Family (Compositae)

Description: The toothed leaves, which have thorns on the margins, alternate on the stem of this 1–5' plant. The 2", pink or pale purple flowers form small tufts.

Bloom Season: June–October

Habitat/Range: In fields and waste places from Newfoundland to North Carolina and from British Columbia to Nebraska and Utah.

Comments: A native of Europe, this plant has become a pesky weed in some northern locations in North America. Given its origins, Canada Thistle is a misnomer, but it is also called California Thistle and in England, Creeping Thistle.

Canada Thistle

FIELD THISTLE
Cirsium discolor
Composite Family (Compositae)

Description: The deeply cut, spiny leaves alternate on the stem of this 3–9' plant and look as if they have white wool on their undersides. The 1½–2" flowers form a pink or light purple head that is broader than that of most common thistles.

Bloom Season: July–November

Habitat/Range: In fields and open, wooded areas from New Brunswick to Ontario and south to Georgia, and in Minnesota, Nebraska, and Missouri.

Comments: Strollers or hikers on the Appalachian Trail from summer to fall from Georgia to Maine will probably notice the Field Thistles in the woods. Its fluffy, bright head stands out among the cool greens, and the flowers are often surrounded by hovering white butterflies. Field Thistle and Tall Thistle *(Cirsium altissimum)* resemble each other, but Tall Thistle is usually found in wet areas and grows taller.

Field Thistle

Bull Thistle

BULL THISTLE
Cirsium vulgare
Composite Family (Compositae)

Description: The divided, prickly leaves alternate on the stem of this 3–6' plant. The bracts are all tipped with spines, and the stem has spines. The 2–3", pink or purple flowers form heads.

Bloom Season: August–September

Habitat/Range: In fields and waste places from Newfoundland to Georgia and also in Minnesota, Oregon, and California. It is a native of Europe, but is also found in Asia.

Comments: This plant is a biennial. One year it simply produces a flat rosette of leaves. The next year the flowering stem can be up to 6' tall.

Purple Coneflower

PURPLE CONEFLOWER
Echinacea purpurea
Composite Family (Compositae)

Description: The broad, lanceolate, slightly toothed leaves alternate on the stem of this 2–4' plant. The 3–4" flowers have a bristly disk and many purple petals.

Bloom Season: June–September

Habitat/Range: In moist, rich soils from Pennsylvania to Georgia.

Comments: Because a popular extract of this plant is used as an herbal remedy to ward off colds, it is possible that more people recognize the botanical name of this plant, *Echinacea,* than the common name, Purple Coneflower.

ELEPHANT'S FOOT OR TOBACCO WEED

Elephantopus carolinianus
Composite Family (Compositae)

Description: The scalloped, ovate leaves grow singly on the stem of this 1–2' plant. The ⅛–¼" purple or blue flowers form small heads that together form what looks like one cluster of flowers.

Bloom Season: August–October

Habitat/Range: In dry open woods from New Jersey to Kansas and south to Florida and Texas.

Comments: Elephant's Foot is mainly a tropical species, and neither the leaves nor flowers of the few plants of this species that grow in North America resemble the feet of an elephant. In late August, Elephant's Foot grows in both the Deep Creek area and the Green Briar Picnic Area of Great Smoky Mountains National Park and along the road near the entrance of the Blue Ridge Parkway in Virginia.

Elephant's Foot or Tobacco Weed

Robin's Plantain

ROBIN'S PLANTAIN

Erigeron pulchellus
Composite Family (Compositae)

Description: The stem leaves are lanceolate and the base leaves have lobes on this 10–18" plant. The leaves are hairy. The 1–1½" flowers have many lilac violet or pink rays and a yellow center disk.

Bloom Season: April–July

Habitat/Range: Fields and open, wooded areas from Maine to Ontario and south to Kansas and Georgia.

Comments: Sometimes called Poor Robin's Plantain, this plant has the showiest and largest flower of all the common fleabanes found in the Appalachian Mountains. It was cultivated in gardens, and like all the other fleabanes, colonists in the 17th century burned it to drive off flies, gnats, and fleas.

Blue Boneset or Mistflower

BLUE BONESET OR MISTFLOWER
Eupatorium coelestinum
Composite Family (Compositae)

Description: The egg-shaped, almost triangular, toothed leaves are opposite each other on the stem of this 1–2' plant. The ¼", blue or violet flowers form a flat cluster.

Bloom Season: July–October

Habitat/Range: In moist soils from New Jersey to Florida and also in the prairie states, the Ozarks, and Texas.

Comments: The flowers resemble a cultivated plant from Mexico called Ageratum *(Ageratum houstonianum)*, and the plant is sometimes called by that name. Mistflowers also grow in the West Indies.

HOLLOW JOE-PYE WEED OR TRUMPETWEED
Eupatorium fistulosum
Composite Family (Compositae)

Description: The toothed, lanceolate leaves have a single vein and form whorls of 4–7 on the stem of this 2–7' plant. The tiny, pink or purple flowers form a domed cluster.

Bloom Season: August–September

Habitat/Range: In moist, open places from New Brunswick south to Georgia.

Comments: Another joe-pye weed with a domed cluster of pink to purplish flowers, Sweet Joe-Pye Weed, or Sweet-Scented Joe-Pye Weed *(Eupatorium purpureum),* also grows in the Appalachian Mountains. Sweet Joe-Pye Weed has only 3 or 4 leaves in the whorl and smells like vanilla when it is bruised.

Hollow Joe-Pye Weed or Trumpetweed

SPOTTED JOE-PYE WEED
Eupatorium maculatum
Composite Family (Compositae)

Description: The lanceolate, toothed leaves form a whorl of 4 or 5 on the stem of this 2–5' plant. The tiny, pink or purple flowers form a flat top cluster.

Bloom Season: August–September

Habitat/Range: In moist soils from Newfoundland to Maryland and in the Great Smoky Mountains.

Comments: In many reference books, the southern range for Spotted Joe-Pye Weed is New York. The plant commonly grows at all elevations in the Smoky Mountain range of the Southern Appalachian Mountains and on the Piedmont in Maryland. This may mean that climates are changing, or it can simply mean the plants were never reported to botanical authorities from those locations.

Spotted Joe-Pye Weed

Blazing Star or Blue Blazing Star

BLAZING STAR OR BLUE BLAZING STAR
Liatris scariosa
Composite Family (Compositae)

Description: The narrow, lanceolate leaves alternate on the stem of this 1–4' plant and get broader toward the bottom of the plant. The bracts have a purple edge. The 1–3" purple flowers have 5 lobed petals and form a dense head.

Bloom Season: July–October

Habitat/Range: In dry woodlands in the Appalachian Mountains from Pennsylvania to Georgia.

Comments: This handsome plant is often cultivated and escapes back to the wild outside the Appalachian Mountains. It is not uncommon to find the plant in parkland near residential areas. In the Southern Appalachian Mountains, *Liatris scariosa* grows along the Blue Ridge Parkway near its Virginia entrance.

SCALY BLAZING STAR
Liatris squarrosa
Composite Family (Compositae)

Description: The lanceolate, entire leaves alternate on the stem of this 10–30" plant. The 1–1½" flower heads are rose purple.

Bloom Season: July–October

Habitat/Range: In dry soils from Delaware to South Dakota and south to Florida and Texas.

Comments: There can be as many as 60 flowers in each head of this blazing star, which grows at low elevations in Great Smoky Mountains National Park.

Scaly Blazing Star

CLIMBING BONESET OR CLIMBING HEMPWEED
Mikania scandens
Composite Family (Compositae)

Description: The triangular or heart-shaped leaves are opposite each other on the stem of this vine. The tiny, white or pinkish flowers form a flat cluster.

Bloom Season: July–October

Habitat/Range: In wet thickets or swamps from southern Ontario south to Florida and Texas.

Comments: Among the composites that grow in the Southern Appalachian Mountains, there are few climbing vines that grow over other plants, so it is usually easy to identify Climbing Hempweed. The common name Climbing Boneset comes from the fact that the flower clusters resemble those of bonesets of the genus *Eupatorium.* Bonesets are usually white and are not vines.

Climbing Boneset or Climbing Hempweed

New York Ironweed

NEW YORK IRONWEED
Vernonia noveboracensis
Composite Family (Compositae)

Description: The lanceolate, toothed leaves alternate on the stem of this 3–6' plant. The ½–1" flowers have 5 purple petals and form tufted heads.

Bloom Season: July–October

Habitat/Range: In moist meadows and near streams and ponds from Massachusetts to Ohio and south to West Virginia and Georgia.

Comments: New York Ironweed grows along the roadsides of Great Smoky Mountains National Park where dripping rocks provide the moist ground this plant needs and also near the streams and marshes of the Cades Cove area. In late August this plant can be seen at many sites along the Blue Ridge Parkway from Virginia to North Carolina.

Ivy-Leaved Morning Glory

IVY-LEAVED MORNING GLORY
Ipomoea hederacea
Morning Glory Family (Convolvulaceae)

Description: The 3-lobed, toothed leaves grow singly on the stem of this vine. The 1–1½" trumpet-shaped flowers have 5 connected white, purple, or blue petals.

Bloom Season: July–October

Habitat/Range: In fields and waste places from Maine to Florida.

Comments: Originally from tropical climates in the Americas, Ivy-Leaved Morning Glory has been naturalized in more northern climates. It grows at low altitudes in Great Smoky Mountains National Park.

LIVE-FOREVER OR ORPINE
Sedum telephium
Orpine Family (Crassulaceae)

Description: The stemless, toothed, ovate, fleshy leaves alternate on the stem of this 8–30" plant. The ¼" flowers have 5 pink or purple petals and form a flat cluster.

Bloom Times: July–September

Habitat/Range: On roadsides and fields. It escaped from cultivation and is found throughout the United States.

Comments: Some field guides list 3 Live-Forevers and others list *Sedum telephium* and discuss whether or not the other 2 are separate species. The others are: *Sedum telephoides,* which often is found growing in open areas of the woods and whose flowers are light pink and leaves less fleshy, and *Sedum purpureum* has red flowers. The more showy plant seen in the illustration grows along the rock outcropping of Skyline Drive in open areas while a light pink version grows in woods along the Appalachian Trail.

Live-Forever or Orpine

Mountain or Catawba Rhododendron

MOUNTAIN RHODODENDRON OR CATAWBA RHODODENDRON
Rhododendron catawbiense
Heath Family (Ericaceae)

Description: The leaves on this 5–20' mountain shrub are entire, lanceolate, dark green, and shiny. The 2–2½" flowers have 5 red or purple petals and form a cluster.

Bloom Season: June–July

Habitat/Range: In mountainous wooded areas from Maryland and southeastern Kentucky to northern Georgia and Alabama.

Comments: From late May to early June, the roads at Great Smoky National Park often have traffic jams due to the spectacular display of blooming rhododendrons. The roads through the Appalachian Mountains of Georgia and Alabama have displays just as spectacular and less traffic.

Pink Azalea or Pinxter Flower

PINK AZALEA OR PINXTER FLOWER
Rhododendron nudiflorum
Heath Family (Ericaceae)

Description: The lanceolate leaves on this 2–10' shrub begin to grow in spring after the plant flowers. The 1½–2" flowers are made up of a pink tube that expands to 5 flaring petals. Five red stamens protrude from the center of the flower.

Bloom Season: April–May

Habitat/Range: In woods and along stream banks and park roads from Massachusetts to Ohio and south to South Carolina and northern Georgia.

Comments: One of several native azaleas, Pinxter Flower blooms in mid-April in Georgia's Chattahoochee National Forest on the La Fayette Ridge Trail and the Pinhotti Trail and in Fort Mountain State Park. In Alabama they can be found in Fort Desoto State Park.

HOG PEANUT
Amphicarpa bracteata
Pea Family (Fabaceae)

Description: The leaves, which alternate on the stem of this vine, are made up of 3 egg-shaped leaflets. The ½–¾" flowers are purple or white and pea shaped.

Bloom Season: August–September

Habitat/Range: In moist thickets from New Brunswick to Florida and west to Manitoba.

Comments: This common vine grows in the Cascade Recreation Area of Jefferson National Forest in Virginia. It is also called Wild Hog Peanut, and although all botanists agree it is a member of the pea family, they disagree on its genus and species.

Hog Peanut

NAKED-FLOWER TICK TREFOIL
Desmodium nudiflorum
Pea Family (Fabaceae)

Description: The leaves, which have 3 pointed, ovate leaflets, are at the base of this 1–3' plant. The ½" rose purple flowers are on a 1–3' separate stem.

Bloom Season: July–September

Habitat/Range: In dry woods from Ontario to Florida.

Comments: It is easy to distinguish this tick trefoil from all the others that grow in the woods. The leafless stem standing by itself with pretty rose purple flowers is unique among tick trefoils.

Naked-Flower Tick Trefoil

Slender Bush Clover

SLENDER BUSH CLOVER
Lespedeza virginica
Pea Family (Fabaceae)

Description: The leaves, which have 3 slender leaflets, alternate on the stem of this 1–3' plant. The ¼–½" purple flowers form clusters in the axil of the leaves.

Bloom Season: August–September

Habitat/Range: In dry soils from New Hampshire to Ontario and south to Arkansas and Florida.

Comments: Bush clovers were planted throughout the eastern United States because hunters believed that they attracted game birds. The plants spread easily, and now several varieties of bush clover grow in open areas.

Kudzu

KUDZU
Pueraria lobata
Pea Family (Fabaceae)

Description: The leaves on this vine are divided into 3 entire, large leaflets. The 1", purple or pink, pea-shaped flowers grow on a stalk.

Bloom Season: August–September

Habitat/Range: This plant from Asia will grow almost anywhere it is planted and spreads easily.

Comments: Kudzu has become a real problem plant, particularly in the southern states. It covers everything on some mountainsides in the Southern Appalachian Mountains. The trees and other native plants beneath the Kudzu die because they cannot get the light they need to make food, and the side of the mountain becomes denuded of all vegetation but the Kudzu.

PINK WILD BEAN
Strophostyles umbellata
Pea Family (Fabaceae)

Description: The leaves on this vine are made up of 3 long, ovate leaflets. The ¾" pink flowers are pea shaped.

Bloom Season: June–October

Habitat/Range: In sandy soils of dry, wooded areas and fields from Long Island south to Florida and Texas.

Comments: This wild bean likes sandy soils and grows at the seashore. In the Southern Appalachian Mountains, it grows in sandy soils in Hungry Mother State Park, Virginia and at low altitudes in Great Smoky Mountains National Park.

Pink Wild Bean

Fringed Gentian

FRINGED GENTIAN
Gentiana crinita
Gentian Family (Gentianaceae)

Description: The stemless, entire, lanceolate leaves are opposite each other on the stem of this 6–18" plant. The 1–2" flowers have 4 purple or blue petals that form a fringed cup.

Bloom Season: August–November

Habitat/Range: In moist meadows, along streams, and in wet wooded areas from Maine to Pennsylvania and south to the mountains of Georgia.

Comments: Although this lovely plant usually has flowers with purple or blue petals, it occasionally produces plants with white or even green flowers. It is often found on the banks of streams and will grow in areas called barrens, which have very poor soils.

Mountain Gentian

MOUNTAIN GENTIAN
Gentiana decora
Gentian Family (Gentianaceae)

Description: The ovate leaves are at the base of this 4–8" plant. The 1–2" blue or purple flowers have 5 lobes that form a closed, pleated tube. The pleats on this gentian are thin and well defined.

Bloom Season: September–October

Habitat/Range: In moist, rich soils from Virginia to Florida.

Comments: Mountain Gentian are often found on the sides of wet cliffs. In the Southern Appalachians there are many roads through state and national parks and the southern part of the Blue Ridge Parkway that are bordered by wet cliffs where Mountain Gentian and other small plants grow in the soil caught in rock depressions.

Long-Stalked Cranesbill

LONG-STALKED CRANESBILL
Geranium columbinum
Geranium Family (Geraniaceae)

Description: The deeply lobed and toothed leaves are opposite each other on the stem of this 6–12" plant. The ½" flowers have 5 rose-purple petals and grow in pairs.

Bloom Season: May–September

Habitat/Range: In fields and on roadsides from New York to Iowa and south to South Carolina and Tennessee.

Comments: A European native transported to the New World, most gardeners now consider Long-Stalked Cranesbill a weed. In late spring, it offers a bright spot of color among plants whose flowers are often pastel.

Wild Geranium

WILD GERANIUM
Geranium maculatum
Geranium Family (Geraniaceae)

Description: The leaves, divided into 3–5 toothed lobes, are opposite each other on the stem of this 1–2' plant. The 1–1½" flowers have 5 red or rose purple petals.

Bloom Season: April–July

Habitat/Range: In woods from Maine to Manitoba and south to Georgia, Alabama, and Wisconsin.

Comments: Wild Geraniums are very common in the eastern United States and can be found in woods almost anywhere there is even a small patch of trees. Cultivated geraniums are usually bred to produce many petals while their wild cousins are much simpler plants. In the Southern Appalachian Mountains, they grow in the Deep Creek area and along River Road in Great Smoky Mountains National Park and in Fort Mountain State Park, Georgia.

DOVE'S FOOT CRANESBILL
Geranium molle
Geranium Family (Geraniaceae)

Description: The lobed, toothed leaves are opposite each other on the stem of this 4–18" plant. The ¼" flowers have 5 rose purple petals.

Bloom Season: June–September

Habitat/Range: In open places from Ontario to Ohio and south to North Carolina and northern Georgia.

Comments: Dove's Foot Cranesbill, a native of Europe, often shows up in lawns, where it is considered a pesky weed. Where the James River goes under the Blue Ridge Parkway, the bright color and interesting shape of Dove's Foot Cranesbill in the grass by the river is eye-catching.

Dove's Foot Cranesbill

FERN-LEAVED PHACELIA OR PURPLE PHACELIA
Phacelia bipinnatifida
Waterleaf Family (Hydrophyllaceae)

Description: The leaves, divided into 5 deeply toothed leaflets, alternate on the stem of this 10–24" plant. The ½–¾" flowers have 5 lavender or blue petals.

Bloom Season: April–May

Habitat/Range: In moist thickets and along streams from Ohio to Illinois and south to Missouri, Georgia, Alabama, and Tennessee.

Comments: In areas with large amounts of rainfall, this phacelia grows along roadsides and trails. Purple Phacelia is abundant in April on both grass-covered roadsides and at the edge of Chestnut Hill Trail in Great Smoky Mountains National Park, where dripping outcrops of rock keep the ground constantly moist.

Fern-Leaved Phacelia or Purple Phacelia

Crested Iris

CRESTED IRIS
Iris cristata
Iris Family (Iridaceae)

Description: The grasslike, 2–3"-wide leaves alternate on the stem of this 2–8" plant. The 1–2" flowers have 3 blue or purple petals with a yellow crest.

Bloom Season: April–May

Habitat/Range: On hillsides and along streams from Maryland to Southern Georgia.

Comments: The crests on the petals help guide insects to the nectar hidden near the reproductive areas of the plant. Look for groups of Crested Iris along the Roaring Fork Motor Nature Trail in Great Smoky Mountains National Park.

Bugle

BUGLE
Ajuga reptans
Mint Family (Labiatae)

Description: The egg-shaped, toothed leaves are opposite each other on the stem of this 6–12" plant. The ½" flowers are blue or purple and the bottom petal forms a lip.

Bloom Season: April–May

Habitat/Range: In fields and along the edges of trails from Maine to Maryland and in the Great Smoky Mountains.

Comments: Another plant naturalized from Europe, it now grows in Great Smoky Mountains National Park in the northeast. In Great Smoky Mountains National Park, it grows along the Turkey Pan Ridge Trail and the Roaring Forks Motor Nature Trail in mid-April.

PURPLE DEAD NETTLE
Lamium purpureum
Mint Family (Labiatae)

Description: The toothed, ovate, scalloped leaves are opposite each other on the stem of this 6–10" plant. The lower leaves are on long stalks. The ⅓–½" flowers have petals that form a lipped purple or red tube. The flowers grow in the axils of the upper leaves, which are on short stalks.

Bloom Season: April–October

Habitat/Range: In fields and on roadsides from Newfoundland to Michigan and south to South Carolina and Missouri.

Comments: Plants that are not true nettles but are called nettle usually have nettlelike leaves. The true nettles *(Urtica)* produce a stinging sensation when brushed against because they have many bristly, stinging hairs.

Purple Dead Nettle

MOTHERWORT
Leonurus cardiaca
Mint Family (Labiatae)

Description: The lobed, toothed leaves are opposite each other on the stem of this 1–3' plant. The pink or purple, ⅛" flowers have a 3-lobed lower lip. The flowers form a circle around the stem.

Bloom Season: July–September

Habitat/Range: In open areas, often near streams or ponds, from Nova Scotia to North Carolina.

Comments: Long ago there was a disease called "Mother" and Motherwort was supposed to be a cure. The term "wort" actually means plant and when placed at the end of the name, it usually means the plant was used medicinally or as a food.

Motherwort

Wild Mint

WILD MINT
Mentha arvensis
Mint Family (Labiatae)

Description: The toothed, ovate leaves are opposite each other on the stem of this 6–18" plant. The ⅛" flowers have 4 light purple petals and are in clusters in the axil of the leaves, encircling the stem.

Bloom Season: July–September

Habitat/Range: In wet or dry wooded areas and on slopes and shores of streams and lakes from Newfoundland to Alaska and south to Virginia, Missouri, and California.

Comments: Sometimes called Field Mint, Wild Mint is a native species. The early colonists applied the leaves to insect bites and stings. Both Native Americans and the colonists made a leaf tea of Wild Mint to treat the symptoms of colds and indigestion. The leaves have a strong mint flavor.

Wild Bergamot

WILD BERGAMOT
Monarda fistulosa
Mint Family (Labiatae)

Description: The sharply toothed, lanceolate leaves are opposite each other on the stem of this 1–3' plant. The 1–1½", light purple, tube-shaped flowers form heads.

Bloom Season: June–September

Habitat/Range: On dry hills and in open wooded areas and thickets from Quebec to Minnesota and south to Virginia. Also in the mountains of Georgia and Tennessee.

Comments: In most parts of the United States where *Monarda* grow, this is the most common species. They grow in large groups, and they spread a minty aroma throughout the area.

CATNIP
Nepeta cataria
Mint Family (Labiatae)

Description: The toothed, heart-shaped leaves have long stalks and are opposite each other on the stem of this 1–3' plant. The ½" flowers are pink and white, the upper petal is slightly hooded, and the lower petal is made up of 3 hanging lobes.

Bloom Season: June–October

Habitat/Range: In open areas and yards practically throughout the United States.

Comments: Catnip was once cultivated because it was believed to have medicinal value. It contains a mild sedative and is still used in folk medicine to alleviate colic in children. It gets its name from the attraction the plant's smell has for cats. Catnip can be found growing near the top of Sharp Mountain in the Peaks of Otter area of the Blue Ridge Parkway in Virginia.

Catnip

BEEFSTEAK PLANT
Perilla frutescens
Mint Family (Labiatae)

Description: The long-stalked, toothed leaves alternate on the stem of this 1–3' plant. The ⅛–¼" pink or white flowers grow along a long stalk.

Bloom Season: September.

Habitat/Range: In open places from Connecticut to Florida.

Comments: A native of India, this plant has escaped from gardens and is cultivated for its foliage, not its flowers. The common name probably comes from the aroma that the plant gives off, which some people describe as rank.

Beefsteak Plant

Heal-All or Selfheal

HEAL-ALL OR SELFHEAL
Prunella vulgaris
Mint Family (Labiatae)

Description: The entire leaves are opposite each other on the stem of this 6–8" plant. The 1–2" flowers are purple, and the petals form a hood and a hanging lip. The flowers grow on a cylindrical head.

Bloom Season: May–September

Habitat/Range: In fields and woods throughout North America.

Comments: In the spring the flower head is usually compact and near the leaves on the stem of the plant. As the summer progresses toward fall, many of the flower heads elongate, get further from the leaves, and make these plants look quite different. Heal-All was supposed to cure an inflammation of the throat called quinsy. It was also valued for curing wounds.

Hoary Mountain Mint

HOARY MOUNTAIN MINT
Pycnanthemum incanum
Mint Family (Labiatae)

Description: The toothed, ovate leaves are opposite each other on the stem of this 1–3' plant. The upper leaves are whitened. The tiny flowers are white or pale lilac and form heads.

Bloom Season: July–September

Habitat/Range: In dry woods and thickets from southern New Hampshire to Illinois and south to Florida.

Comments: Hoary Mountain Mint can be found along the Blue Ridge Parkway in Virginia around the Peaks of Otter, both on the roadside and on the nature trail near the visitors center. It can also be found along the roadsides on the Tennessee side of Great Smoky Mountains National Park.

LYRE-LEAVED SAGE
Salvia lyrata
Mint Family (Labiatae)

Description: The lobed base leaves form a roseate, and the lanceolate stem leaves are opposite each other on the stem of this 1–2' plant. The 1" flowers are purple and tubular.

Bloom Season: April–June

Habitat/Range: In sandy woods from Connecticut to Missouri and south to Florida and Texas.

Comments: Lyre-Leaved Sage is native to the United States. The cultivated sage used in cooking *(Salvia officinalis)* is a European native with red flowers. Lyre-Leaved Sage can be found in April on the La Fayette Ridge Trail in Chattahoochee National Forest and in Floyd Jones State Park and Fort Mountain State Park, all in Georgia.

Lyre-Leaved Sage

Maddog Skullcap

MADDOG SKULLCAP
Scutellaria lateriflora
Mint Family (Labiatae)

Description: The toothed, ovate leaves are opposite each other on the stem of this 6–30" plant. The ½" violet and white flowers are in the shape of a hooded tube and are all on one side of the stem.

Bloom Season: June–September

Habitat/Range: In wet wooded areas, thickets, and meadows from Quebec to British Columbia and south to Florida and California.

Comments: The leaf shape can vary and the leaves can almost have a triangular shape. The common name of the plant comes from a belief that the plant had an efficacy against rabies. It was also supposed to cure hysteria.

Nodding Wild Onion

NODDING WILD ONION
Allium cernuum
Lily Family (Lilliaceae)

Description: The long, narrow, grasslike leaves are at the base of this 8–18" plant. The ¼" flowers have 6 pink or white petals. The flowers form a head, and the head of the plant nods.

Bloom Season: June–September

Habitat/Range: In fields and on hillsides and stream banks from New York to Minnesota south to Tennessee, and in the Rocky Mountains.

Comments: Another plant of the lily family, Wild Leek or Ramps *(Allium tricoccum)*, grows in the Southern Appalachian Mountains. It has a similar but erect flowering head. Like Nodding Wild Onion, it gives off the familiar smell of commercially sold onions and garlic. Ramps are still gathered and used today. The leaves of Ramps, which are much wider, do not appear until after the flower bloom fades.

GRAPE HYACINTH
Muscari botryoides
Lily Family (Lilliaceae)

Description: The grasslike, fleshy leaves are at the base of this 3–8" plant. The ⅛" flowers have 6 purple or blue petals that form a globe. The small globes form a pyramidal cluster.

Bloom Season: April–May

Habitat/Range: In areas near once-settled land throughout the United States.

Comments: This European plant is widely cultivated and has escaped to the wild. It can be found in April in the Cades Cove area of Great Smoky Mountains National Park.

Grape Hyacinth

Catesby's Trillium

VICTOR MEDINA

CATESBY'S TRILLIUM
Trillium catesbaei
Lily Family (Lilliaceae)

Description: The 3 lanceolate leaves form a whorl on the stem of this 6–12" plant. The 1½" flowers have 3 pink or white reflexed petals and prominent yellow stamens.

Bloom Season: April–May

Habitat/Range: In the wooded areas and forests on the Piedmont and lower elevations in the mountains of the southeastern United States.

Comments: The Appalachian Mountain range has its southern terminus in northwestern Georgia and northeastern Alabama. This end of the range is the perfect location for this very pretty trillium, and by mid-April it is abundant in the state parks and national forests in both states.

Great Lobelia or Blue Lobelia

GREAT LOBELIA OR BLUE LOBELIA
Lobelia siphilitica
Lobelia Family (Lobeliodeae)

Description: The toothed leaves alternate on the stem of this 1–3' plant. The 1–1½" flowers are purple or blue with a lower lip that is divided into 3 points with white markings. The upper lip is 2 erect teeth.

Bloom Season: August–September

Habitat/Range: On wet land, roadsides, and along streams from Maine to Manitoba and south to North Carolina, Alabama, and Texas.

Comments: The species name, *siphilitica,* indicates that it was once believed that this plant could cure syphilis. It was supposed to be a secret remedy of Native Americans. Great Lobelia can be found in the Deep Creek area of Great Smoky Mountains National Park and in the Peaks of Otter area of the Blue Ridge Parkway.

MEADOW BEAUTY OR DEERGRASS
Rhexia virginica
Meadow-Beauty (Melastomataceae)

Description: The toothed, stemless, hairy, ovate leaves are opposite each other on the stem of this 6–24" plant. The 1" flowers have 4 purplish red reflexed petals and bright yellow stamens.

Bloom Season: July–September

Habitat/Range: In wet, sandy, and peaty places from Nova Scotia to Ontario and south to Florida.

Comments: Two Meadow Beauty plants grow in the Southern Appalachian Mountains. Maryland Meadow Beauty *(Rhexia mariana)* has pink flowers and the leaves have stalks.

Meadow Beauty or Deergrass

FIREWEED OR GREAT WILLOW HERB
Epilobium angustifolium
Evening Primrose Family (Onagraceae)

Description: The entire, lanceolate leaves alternate on the stem of this 3–8' plant. The 1–2" flowers have 4 magenta petals and are in a terminal spike.

Bloom Season: June–September

Habitat/Range: In dry soil from Greenland to Alaska and south to New Hampshire in the Appalachian Mountains and to Arizona and California on the West Coast. Also found in the Appalachian Mountains of North Carolina and Tennessee.

Comments: It also grows in England where it first appeared along railroads and new roads after the Industrial Revolution, and it grew all over London after the bombings of World War II. The American Indians called it wickiup or wickopy, perhaps because this plant and others called by the same name were used in the construction of shelters called wickiups.

Fireweed or Great Willow Herb

Pink Lady's Slipper or Moccasin-Flower

PINK LADY'S SLIPPER OR MOCCASIN-FLOWER
Cypripedium acaule
Orchid Family (Orchidaceae)

Description: The 2 elongated, ovate leaves are at the base of this 8–12" plant. The 1–3" flowers have a pink to reddish cleft pouch.

Bloom Season: April–July

Habitat/Range: In dry or moist wooded areas and bogs from Newfoundland to Alberta and south to Georgia, Alabama, and Minnesota.

Comments: Lady's Slipper's botanical name *(Cypripedium)* refers to the sandal or slipper *(pedilum)* of Aphrodite, the goddess of love and beauty who was born on the island of Cyprus. Aphrodite is the Greek goddess of love, and Venus is her Roman equivalent. Since Cyprus has belonged to both Greece and Rome, the flower is sometimes referred to as Venus Slipper. Pink Lady's Slipper can be found in mid-April on the Red Blaze Trail in Fort Mountain State Park, Georgia, and the Red Blaze Trail in Fort Desoto State Park, Alabama.

Violet Wood Sorrel

VIOLET WOOD SORREL
Oxalis violacea
Wood-Sorrel Family (Oxalidaceae)

Description: The leaves, made up of 3-lobed leaflets, are at the base of this 4–8" plant and often are green with a purple outline. The ¾–1" flowers have 5 violet or purple petals.

Bloom Season: April–July

Habitat/Range: In open, wooded areas, fields, and prairies from Massachusetts to Minnesota and Colorado and south to Florida and Texas.

Comments: The undersides of the leaves are usually purple, and a wind can turn a green-looking field to purple in a second. Violet Wood Sorrel can be found as early as mid-April in Fort Mountain State Park, Georgia, and the Cades Cove area of Smoky Mountains National Park.

Passion Flower

PASSION FLOWER
Passiflora incarnata
Passion-Flower Family (Passifloraceae)

Description: The leaves on this vine have 3–5 lobes that each come to a point. The 2–3" flowers have white, pink, and purple petals.

Bloom Season: June–September

Habitat/Range: In thickets and along hedges from Maryland to Missouri and Oklahoma and south to Florida and Texas.

Comments: Among the early European explorers of the southern United States were priests who saw in this unfamiliar and beautiful flower the crown of thorns of the crucifixion. They gave the flower its name. Passion Flower can be seen blooming in August around the Peaks of Otter section of the Blue Ridge Parkway.

Smooth Phlox

SMOOTH PHLOX
Phlox glaberrima
Phlox Family (Polemoniaceae)

Description: The long, lanceolate, and pointed leaves are opposite each other on the stem of this 1–5' plant. The 1–1½" flowers have 5 pink or purple petals.

Bloom Season: May–July

Habitat/Range: In wet wooded areas and thickets from Ohio to Wisconsin and south to Florida and Texas.

Comments: There are usually a great many flowers at the top of each plant and its height makes this plant stand out. It can be found blooming along the Mountain to Sea Trail off the Blue Ridge Parkway in North Carolina.

DOWNY PHLOX
Phlox pilosa
Phlox Family (Polemoniaceae)

Description: The entire, lanceolate, and stalkless leaves are opposite each other on the downy stem of this 6–18" plant. The 1–1½" flowers have 5 white, pink, or purple petals. The petals on this phlox are not notched.

Bloom Season: April–May

Habitat/Range: In dry soils from Maine to Manitoba and south to Florida, Arkansas, and Texas.

Comments: In mid-April Downy Phlox can be found along the La Fayette Ridge Trail in Georgia's Chattahoochee National Forest. Downy refers to the stem, which is usually soft and hairy.

Victor Medina

Downy Phlox

Moss Phlox or Moss Pink

MOSS PHLOX OR MOSS PINK
Phlox subulata
Phlox Family (Polemoniaceae)

Description: The leaves, divided into narrow leaflets, alternate on the stem of this sprawling plant. The ½–1" flowers have 5 white, rose, or violet notched petals.

Bloom Season: March–May

Habitat/Range: In dry, sandy, or rocky soils from New York to Florida.

Comments: Moss Phlox is cultivated, commonly found on front lawns with steep slopes or in rock gardens.

Fringed Polygala or Gaywings

FRINGED POLYGALA OR GAYWINGS
Polygala paucifolia
Milkwort Family (Polygalaceae)

Description: The egg-shaped leaves alternate on the stem of this 3–5" plant. The ¾" reddish or purplish flower has a center tube and 2 tubes perpendicular to the center tube. The side tubes are actually sepals fringed with petals.

Bloom Season: April–June

Habitat/Range: In woods with acid soils from Ontario to Manitoba and south to Georgia.

Comments: This spring plant blooms from mid-April to early May in the Southern Appalachian Mountains and in mid-May to early June in northern Pennsylvania. In mid-April Gaywings bloom along the trail from the parking lot in Hungry Mother State Park and in the Cascade Recreation Area of Jefferson National Forest in southwestern Virginia.

PURPLE MILKWORT OR FIELD MILKWORT
Polygala sanguinea
Milkwort Family (Polygalaceae)

Description: The lanceolate, entire leaves alternate on the stem of this 6–12" plant. The tiny flowers form heads and vary from pink to green or white.

Bloom Season: June–October

Habitat/Range: In meadows and fields from Nova Scotia to Minnesota and south to South Carolina and Oklahoma.

Comments: The name milkwort comes from the once held belief that if cows ate certain plants of this species it would increase their milk production. Purple Milkwort can be seen around the 200-mile area of the Blue Ridge Parkway in North Carolina.

Purple Milkwort or Field Milkwort

PINK SMARTWEED

Polygonum pensylvanicum
Buckwheat Family (Polygonaceae)

Description: The grasslike, shiny leaves alternate on the stem of this 1–4' plant. The tiny flowers are pink or white and in erect spikes. Each flower has 5 petals.

Bloom Season: June–October

Habitat/Range: In wet places and along streams from Quebec to Minnesota and south to Florida and Texas.

Comments: The flowers are usually pink and the plant can grow unusually tall for a smartweed. Pink Smartweed can be found at low altitudes in Smoky Mountains National Park.

Pink Smartweed

Arrow-Leaved Tearthumb

ARROW-LEAVED TEARTHUMB

Polygonum sagittatum
Buckwheat Family (Polygonaceae)

Description: The arrowhead-shaped leaves alternate on the stem of this vine. The ¼", white or rose-colored flowers form small heads. The stem of the plant is covered with prickles (soft, small thorns), which is why these vines are called tearthumbs.

Bloom Season: July–September

Habitat/Range: In moist soils from Nova Scotia south to Kansas and Florida.

Comments: The related Halberd-Leaved Tearthumb *(Polygonum arifolium)* also grows in the Appalachian Mountains. Its leaf looks like the points of the arrow have been pulled sideways.

Mountain Spiderwort

MOUNTAIN SPIDERWORT
Tradescantia subaspera var. *montana*
Pickerelweed Family (Pontederiaceae)

Description: The lanceolate leaves alternate (spiderlike) on the stem of this plant. The 1–2", 3-petal, purple flowers have a center ring of 6 yellow stamens.

Bloom Season: June–August

Habitat/Range: In woods and thickets of the mountains from southwestern Virginia to Georgia.

Comments: Spiderworts have a strange property. They open in the morning, and if they are pollinated, the petals wilt and moisture appears. Mountain Spiderwort grows in the area where the James River flows under the Blue Ridge Parkway in Virginia.

ROCKET LARKSPUR
Delphinium ajacis
Buttercup Family (Ranunculaceae)

Description: The leaves are finely divided into thin strands and alternate on the stem of this 1–3' plant. The 1–1½" flowers have 5 blue or purplish petals and a spur at the rear of the flower.

Bloom Season: June–August

Habitat/Range: Along roadsides and in fields near areas that have once been settled.

Comments: Rocket Larkspur is native to Europe and is an escapee from gardens. Dwarf Larkspur *(Delphinium tricorne)* also grows in the Southern Appalachian Mountains. It has a similar flower, but the leaves are divided into 2–5 not deeply divided sections, each one lobed into 3 or 4 parts. The plant rarely reaches 2' and blooms in spring. All parts of the *Delphinium* plants are poisonous.

Rocket Larkspur

Sharp-Lobed Hepatica

SHARP-LOBED HEPATICA
Hepatica acutiloba
Buttercup Family (Ranunculaceae)

Description: The leaves have 3 pointed lobes and are at the base of this 3–8" plant. When the flowers bloom there may be some old leaves from last year. New leaves usually start to grow as the flowers die off. The ½–1" flowers have 6–12 white, blue, or pink petal-like sepals. There can be several different colored flowers in each group.

Bloom Season: March–May

Habitat/Range: One of the earliest blooms of spring in rich, wooded areas, often near streams, from Nova Scotia south to Florida.

Comments: Round-Lobed Hepatica or Liverleaf *(Hepatica americana)* also grows in the Appalachian Mountains. The difference between the 2 plants is in the shape of their leaves, as the common name indicates. By early April, only the leaves of both the hepaticas cover hillsides of the Southern Appalachian Mountains.

Carolina Rose or Pasture Rose

CAROLINA ROSE OR PASTURE ROSE
Rosa carolina
Rose Family (Rosaceae)

Description: The leaf is divided into 8–10 ovate, toothed leaflets, and all but the top one are opposite each other. The shrub grows to 1–3'. The 1½–2" flowers have 5 pink petals and prominent yellow stamens in the center. The stem has 2-pronged, straight thorns below the leaf axil.

Bloom Season: May–July

Habitat/Range: In dry, open, wooded areas, meadows, and pastures from Nova Scotia to Minnesota and south to Florida and Texas.

Comments: The pink wild roses that grow in the Southern Appalachian Mountains are distinguishable only by the number of leaflets in the leaf or how the thorn is placed below the leaf axil. At least one other pink rose, Swamp Rose *(Rosa palustris)*, is commonly found in Great Smoky Mountains National Park.

PURPLE-FLOWERING RASPBERRY OR MAPLE-LEAVED RASPBERRY
Rubus odoratus
Rose Family (Rosaceae)

Description: The 5 toothed and lobed leaves alternate on the stem of this 3–6' shrub. The 1–2" flowers have 5 rose purple petals.

Bloom Season: June–August

Habitat/Range: In rocky woods from Nova Scotia to Ontario and Michigan and south to Georgia and Tennessee.

Comments: This raspberry often grows in the rocky hillsides above streams and rivers. The berries are edible but not as tasty as other wild raspberries such as the Red Wild Raspberry *(Rubus idaeus)* that grow in the Appalachian Mountains.

Purple-Flowering Raspberry or Maple-Leaved Raspberry

Purple Gerardia

PURPLE GERARDIA
Agalinis purpurea
Snapdragon Family (Scrophulariaceae)

Description: The grasslike leaves are opposite each other on the stem of this 10–30" plant. The 1–1½" flowers have 5 purple petals that form a flaring tube.

Bloom Season: June–September

Habitat/Range: In damp places from southern New England to Nebraska and south to Florida and Texas.

Comments: Gerardia differ from each other in where they grow, the size of the flower, and the shape of the leaf. Another gerardia, Slender Gerardia *(Agalinis tenuifolia),* grows in dry soils at low and middle altitudes in Great Smoky Mountains National Park. This plant is 6–20" and its flowers are ½" or less.

Pink Turtlehead

PINK TURTLEHEAD
Chelone obliqua
Snapdragon Family (Scrophulariaceae)

Description: The toothed leaves are opposite each other on the stem of this 1–3' plant. The 1–2" flowers are pink and form a lipped tube.

Bloom Season: July–September

Habitat/Range: In moist soils from Maryland to Indiana and south to Florida and Texas.

Comments: The flowers of the turtleheads closely resemble the heads of turtles. Pink Turtlehead can be found in August in the Cades Cove area of Great Smoky Mountains National Park.

SQUARE STEMMED MONKEY FLOWER
Mimulus ringens
Snapdragon Family (Scrophulariaceae)

Description: The toothed, lanceolate, stalked leaves are opposite each other on the stem of this 1–3' plant. The 1" flowers are on long stalks and have 3 violet or pink petals and a yellow center. The bottom petal hangs down and has a notch.

Bloom Season: June–September

Habitat/Range: In swamps and along lakefronts and stream banks from Nova Scotia to Virginia and in Tennessee and North Carolina.

Square Stemmed Monkey Flower

Comments: Winged Monkey Flower *(Mimulus alatus)* is another monkey flower that grows in the Appalachian Mountains. The flowers are similar to this monkey flower but have no or very small stalks and are on either side of the stem of the plant.

GRAY BEARDTONGUE
Penstemon canescens
Snapdragon Family (Scrophulariaceae)

Gray Beardtongue

Description: The lanceolate, toothed leaves have no stalk and are opposite each other on the stem of this 1–3' plant. The 1½" flowers have 5 pale purple petals and a flattened trumpet shape.

Bloom Season: May–August

Habitat/Range: In and at the edge of dry, wooded areas and on rocky outcrops, chiefly in the hills and mountains from Pennsylvania to Indiana and southward to Georgia and Alabama.

Comments: Gray Beardtongue is a common plant blooming on many of the rocky outcrops along Chimney Top Nature Trail in Great Smoky Mountains National Park. Hairy Beardtongue *(Penstemon hirsutus)*, which has small hairs on its stem and leaves and a wider mouth flower, grows on the Chimney Top trail.

Horse Nettle

HORSE NETTLE
Solanum carolinense
Potato Family (Solanaceae)

Description: The lobed, toothed leaves alternate on the stem of this 1–4' plant. The leaves have prickles on the lower sides along the mid-rib. The 1–1½", star-shaped flowers have 5 purple or white petals and prominent yellow stamens in the center.

Bloom Season: May–October

Habitat/Range: In open areas from New England to Washington and south to Florida and Texas.

Comments: Horse Nettles have eye-catching flowers, but the plant is considered a pest because of the prickles on the stems and the leaves. Horse Nettles grow in August around mile 200 on the Blue Ridge Parkway and on Clingman's Dome in Great Smoky Mountains National Park.

Marsh Blue Violet

MARSH BLUE VIOLET
Viola cucullata
Violet Family (Violacaea)

Description: The heart-shaped leaves are at the base of this 6–10" plant. The ¾–1" flowers are purple with a white center. Each flower has 5 petals, 3 of which form a lip. The flower has a spur at the rear of the top 2 petals.

Bloom Season: April–May

Habitat/Range: In wet places from Quebec to Ontario and south to the mountains of Georgia.

Comments: The petals are darker toward the center, and the flower usually grows on a separate stem rising above the leaves. Southern Wood Violet *(Viola hirsutula)* grows in dry places and has similar leaves on a separate stem, but the backs of the leaves are reddish or purple. Southern Wood Violet can be found on Chestnut Hill in Great Smoky Mountains National Park, while the Marsh Blue Violet is usually found beside streams and in marshy ground.

COMMON BLUE VIOLET
Viola papilionacea
Violet Family (Violacaea)

Description: The heart-shaped, toothed leaves are at the base of the plant separate from the stem on which the flower grows. The plant is 4–8" high. The ¾–1" flowers have 5 purple, purple and white, or all-white petals. The lower 3 petals form a lip for the flower.

Bloom Season: April–June

Habitat/Range: In moist meadows and groves from Massachusetts to Minnesota and south to Florida.

Comments: The purple-and-white variety of the common violet is cultivated and is often called Confederate Ladies or Confederate Violet. Common Blue Violet is found in Georgia in both the Sosebee Cove area of Chattahoochee National Forest and on the Fort Mountain State Park Nature Trail.

Common Blue Violet

Birdfoot Violet

BIRDFOOT VIOLET
Viola pedata
Violet Family (Violacaea)

Description: The leaves are divided into 5 parts and are at the base of this 6–8" plant. The ¾" flowers have 5 lavender petals that have a yellow center. Some Birdfoot Violets have a dark purple bottom petal.

Bloom Season: April–June

Habitat/Range: In fields, on banks, and in woods from Massachusetts to Minnesota and south to Florida and Louisiana.

Comments: This plant is called Birdfoot or Crowfoot Violet because the leaves resemble the shape of a bird's foot. This is the showiest of the wild violets, and its most showy form—with a deep purple bottom petal—is more often seen in the Southern Appalachian Mountains and on a rock outcrop around mile 90 on the Blue Ridge Parkway in Virginia. A violet with a white center and not so deeply cut 5-lobed leaves, Coast Violet *(Viola brittoniana)*, grows in the Sandstone Falls area of West Virginia.

RED FLOWERS

Toadshade Trillium

Trumpet or Coral Honeysuckle

TRUMPET OR CORAL HONEYSUCKLE
Lonicera sempervirens
Honeysuckle Family (Caprifoliaceae)

Description: The ovate leaves are opposite each other on this vine. The smooth leaves are below the whorl of flowers and actually joined together around the stem of the vine. The 1–2" flowers have 5 scarlet petals that form a tube that flares and often shows a yellow tip. The flowers can be all yellow but they are most often a whorl of red, flared tubes with a yellow lip.

Bloom Season: April–September

Habitat/Range: In woods and thickets from Maine to Iowa and south to Florida and Texas.

Comments: Trumpet Honeysuckle grow mostly at the edges of woods on the Piedmont and the Coastal Plain in southern states, but they are also found at low altitudes in Great Smoky Mountains National Park.

FIRE PINK
Silene virginica
Pink Family (Caryophyllaceae)

Description: The lanceolate leaves are opposite each other on the stem of this 6–18" plant. The 1–1½" flowers have 5 toothed scarlet petals.

Bloom Season: April–September

Habitat/Range: On road- and trailsides and in woodlands from western New York and southwestern Ontario to Minnesota and south to Georgia and Missouri.

Comments: By mid-April, Fire Pinks can be found along the Blue Ridge Parkway near Otters Creek, along the roadsides of Great Smoky Mountains National Park, and in Fort Mountain State Park in Georgia. By May they can be found in Cacapon State Park in West Virginia, which is in the Central Appalachian Mountains.

Fire Pink

SWEET BETSY OR SWEET SHRUB
Calycanthus floridus
Laurel Family (Ericaceae)

Description: The leaves on this 6–8' shrub are ovate. The 1–2" flowers grow in pairs and have many brownish red or maroon petals.

Bloom Season: April–May

Habitat/Range: In woods and thickets from Virginia south to Alabama and Florida.

Comments: Sweet Betsy, also called Hairy Strawberry Shrub, blooms in mid-April on the La Fayette Ridge Trail in the Chattahoochee National Forest and on the nature trail in Fort Mountain State Park in Georgia, in Alabama at Fort Desoto State Park on the first trail that bisects the Red Blaze Trail, and many other locations in the woods and thickets of the Southern Appalachian Mountains.

Sweet Betsy or Sweet Shrub

Redbud

REDBUD
Cercis canadensis
Pea Family (Fabaceae)

Description: The heart-shaped leaves are not on this 6–12' small tree or shrub when it flowers. The ⅓" pea-shaped flowers are deep pink or rose red.

Bloom Season: April–May

Habitat/Range: In rich soils from Ontario to New York and south to Florida. Also in Texas.

Comments: In April the blooming Redbuds create a spectacular sight along the highways through the Shenandoah Valley in Virginia. They can also be seen along the Blue Ridge Parkway in both Virginia and North Carolina, along River Road in Great Smoky Mountains National Park in Tennessee, and in Hungry Mother State Park in Virginia.

Crimson or Italian Clover

CRIMSON OR ITALIAN CLOVER
Trifolium incarnatum
Pea Family (Fabaceae)

Description: The leaves, which alternate on the stem of this 6–24" plant, are made up of 3 blunt-ended leaflets. The 1½–2½" flowers are crimson or deep red and form a cylindrical head.

Bloom Season: April–July

Habitat/Range: In fields and on roadsides found near areas that were once cultivated.

Comments: Crimson Clover is a native of Europe and is cultivated in the United States for its bright color. The flowers are soft and downy. The plant blooms at low altitudes in Great Smoky Mountains National Park in late April.

BEE BALM OR OSWEGO-TEA
Monarda didyma
Mint Family (Labiatae)

Description: The short-stalked, lanceolate, and toothed leaves are opposite one another on the square stem of this 1–2' plant. The 1–3" flower heads are red and the petals tubular. The bracts are often reddish.

Bloom Season: June–September

Habitat/Range: In wet fields and along stream banks from Quebec to Michigan and south to Georgia and Tennessee.

Comments: Native Americans often made leaf tea from Bee Balm to treat colic and gas. Although the normal blooming period of the plant usually ends sometime in September, the plant can be found blooming as late as October on the mile-high Clingmans Dome Road in Great Smoky National Park on the North Carolina-Tennessee border.

Bee Balm or Oswego-Tea

TOADSHADE TRILLIUM
Trillium sessile
Lily Family (Lilliaceae)

Description: The ovate, spotted leaves form a whorl of 3 on the stem of this 4–12" plant. The 1–2" flowers have 3 red or green petals and appear to be an unopened bud.

Bloom Season: April–May

Habitat/Range: In moist woods from Pennsylvania to Ohio and Minnesota and south to Florida and Mississippi.

Comments: Also called Sessile Flowered Wake Robin, this plant can be found in late April and early May in the woods of Georgia's Fort Mountain State Park and Chattahoochee National Forest.

Toadshade Trillium

Cardinal Flower

CARDINAL FLOWER
Lobelia cardinalis
Lobelia Family (Lobeliodeae)

Description: The lanceolate, toothed leaves alternate on the stem of this 1–3' plant. The ½–1" scarlet flowers have a lower lip that is split most of the way into 3 parts. The upper lip of the flower has a split through which the white stamen protrudes.

Bloom Season: July–September

Habitat/Range: In moist soils along stream banks, ponds, and lakes and in wet meadows from Newfoundland to North Carolina.

Comments: Cardinal Flowers grow on the grassy shoulders of the roadways that wind through the valleys of Great Smoky Mountains National Park due to the abundant rainfall. Moisture drips off the cliffs overhanging the roads and provides the plants with just the type of environment they need. Cardinal Flowers also grow along streams and under overhangs on the Blue Ridge Parkway.

WILD BLEEDING HEART OR FRINGED BLEEDING HEART
Dicentra eximia
Poppy Family (Papaveraceae)

Description: The finely divided leaves are at the base of this 8–18" plant. The 1–1½" flowers have 2 dark pink or red spurs.

Bloom Season: April–September

Habitat/Range: On rocky ledges in wooded, mountainous areas from New York southward and southwest to Georgia and Tennessee.

Comments: This plant is native to the Appalachian Mountains, and it is sometimes cultivated. The usual garden bleeding heart *(Dicentra spectabilis)* is a native of Asia. Wild Bleeding Heart grows in Virginia near the trail that runs through Beartree Recreation Area of Jefferson National Forest and near the top of Sharp Mountain at Peaks of Otter on the Blue Ridge Parkway.

Wild Bleeding Heart or Fringed Bleeding Heart

SCARLET PIMPERNEL OR POOR MAN'S WEATHERGLASS
Anagallis arvensis
Primrose Family (Primulaceae)

Description: The stemless, ovate leaves are opposite each other on the stem of this sprawling plant. The ½" flowers have 5 red or orange-red petals. The plants with orange-red petals have a red ring in the center of the plant's petals.

Bloom Season: May–August

Habitat/Range: In fields and open places practically throughout North America.

Comments: The plant is a European native. The flowers close at the approach of poor weather, which is why the English call it Poor Man's Weatherglass. In Ireland it is believed to be a magic plant that one only has to hold to understand the language of birds.

VICTOR MEDINA

Scarlet Pimpernel or Poor Man's Weatherglass

Columbine

COLUMBINE
Aquilegia canadensis
Buttercup Family (Ranunculaceae)

Description: The leaves have 3 lobed leaflets and alternate on the stem of this 1–3' plant. The 1–1½" flowers have 5 red spurs that form a crown. The crown has a yellow center and yellow dangling stamen.

Bloom Season: April–August

Habitat/Range: From Nova Scotia to the Northwest Territories and south to Florida and Texas.

Comments: Columbine can be seen in mid-April on the hillsides and rock outcrops that line the roads of Great Smoky Mountains National Park. The same display can be seen around the summer solstice in June on Skyline Drive in Shenandoah National Park in northern Virginia and by early July along the roads of the northern mountains of Pennsylvania.

Clematis or Leatherflower

CLEMATIS OR LEATHERFLOWER
Clematis viorna
Buttercup Family (Ranunculaceae)

Description: The leaves have 3–7 toothed leaflets and are opposite on the stem of this vine. The 1–1½", bowler-hat shaped flowers have 4 reddish or purple petals that terminate in a white turned-up border.

Bloom Season: June

Habitat/Range: On banks and in thickets from southern Pennsylvania to Georgia.

Comments: The bowler-hat shaped flower on this vine is very different in appearance from most other wild and cultivated clematis. The confirmation that it is a clematis comes when the seeds form and they have the feathery appearance of all other clematis vine seeds.

Lousewort or Wood Betony

LOUSEWORT OR WOOD BETONY
Pedicularis canadensis
Snapdragon Family (Scrophulariaceae)

Description: The deeply notched leaves alternate on the stem of this ½–1½' plant. The ½" flowers form an array of yellow or reddish bent tubes, each with 4 lobes.

Bloom Season: April–June

Habitat/Range: In dry woods and thickets from Nova Scotia to Manitoba and south to Florida, Mississippi, and Colorado.

Comments: This plant blooms in April in mountainous areas of southern states. From the northern Virginia mountains north, it blooms in June. It can be found blooming in mid-April in Hungry Mother State Park in Virginia and along River Road in Great Smoky Mountains National Park in Tennessee. The plant's name comes from the mistaken belief that cattle who grazed in fields where European Lousewort grew would become infested with lice.

BLUE FLOWERS

Wild Hyacinth

Vipers Bugloss or Blue Weed

VICTOR MEDINA

VIPERS BUGLOSS OR BLUE WEED
Echium vulgare
Borage Family (Boraginaceae)

Description: The lanceolate leaves alternate on the stem of this 1½–2' plant. The 1–2" blue flowers have an extended bottom lip and protruding bright red stamens. The flowers bloom in one-sided spikes.

Bloom Season: June–October

Habitat/Range: In open places from Nova Scotia to North Carolina and in Ontario and Nebraska.

Comments: Naturalized from Europe, this is a troublesome plant in some northern areas. It grows at mid-level altitudes in Great Smoky Mountains National Park and near the lookouts along the Blue Ridge Parkway.

TALL BELLFLOWER
Campanula americana
Bluebell Family (Campanulaceae)

Description: The lanceolate, toothed leaves alternate on the stem of this 1–4' plant. The ¾–1" flowers have 5 light blue petals. The star-shaped flowers have 3 stigma on top of a prominent, long style.

Bloom Season: June–September

Habitat/Range: In moist woods from New Brunswick to South Dakota and south to Florida and Kansas.

Comments: Tall Bellflower is the only species in this family with bell-like flowers. Look for it on open slopes off the Blue Ridge Parkway and in Great Smoky Mountains National Park.

Tall Bellflower

Southern Harebell or Bellflower

SOUTHERN HAREBELL OR BELLFLOWER
Campanula divaricata
Bluebell Family (Campanulaceae)

Description: The lanceolate, toothed leaves alternate on the stem of this 1–3' plant. The ⅓" flowers have 5 blue petals shaped into a hanging bell. There are many flowers on one plant.

Bloom Season: July–September

Habitat/Range: In dry woods and rocky cliffs from the Piedmont in Maryland south to Kentucky and Georgia.

Comments: Southern Harebell is a very common flower in the Southern Appalachian Mountains. It usually grows under the dry outcrops along the Blue Ridge Parkway, in Hungry Mother State Park in Virginia and along the nature trail at the Chimney Top Picnic Area in Great Smoky Mountains National Park.

Chicory

CHICORY
Cichorium intybus
Composite Family (Compositae)

Description: The toothed leaves alternate on the stem of this 1–4' plant. The 1–2" blue or white flower petals have a straight end like a dandelion. The flowers grow on a long, almost bare stem.

Bloom Season: June–October

Habitat/Range: In fields and meadows and along roadsides from Nova Scotia to Minnesota and south to North Carolina and Kansas. Also in Colorado and California.

Comments: Continuing a practice that began in Holland in the 18th century when coffee was extremely expensive, chicory root is still roasted and mixed with or substituted for coffee. Grown under special conditions by commercial growers, the broad-leaved variety is the high-priced green sold as Belgian endive.

WILD HYACINTH OR EASTERN CAMASS
Camassia scilloides
Lily Family (Lilliaceae)

Description: The wide, grasslike leaves are at the base of this 1–2' plant. The ½–¾" flowers have 6 blue petals and a small yellow center disk surrounded by stamens.

Bloom Season: April–June

Habitat/Range: In meadows and along streams from western Pennsylvania to Minnesota and south to Georgia and Texas.

Comments: It is unusual for flowers in the lily family to be blue. The range of the plant indicates that it is more likely to be found in the Southern Appalachian Mountains of Tennessee, Georgia, or Alabama. The genus name *Camassia* is derived from the Native Americans name, quamash, for these bulbs. There are several western species.

Wild Hyacinth or Eastern Camass

BLUE PHLOX OR WILD BLUE PHLOX
Phlox divaricata
Phlox Family (Polemoniaceae)

Description: The lanceolate, entire leaves are opposite each other on the stem of this 8–18" plant. The 1–1½" flowers have 5 blue or white petals around the top of a flaring tube.

Bloom Season: April–June

Habitat/Range: In moist woods from Ontario to Minnesota and south to Florida and Louisiana.

Comments: In April Wild Blue Phlox is plentiful in the Cascade Recreation Area of the Jefferson National Forest of Southwestern Virginia, on the Blue Ridge Parkway, and on the Tennessee side of Great Smoky Mountains National Park along the Visitors Center Nature Trail and on the North Carolina side in the Deep Creek area.

Blue Phlox or Wild Blue Phlox

Greek Valerian or Jacob's Ladder

GREEK VALERIAN OR JACOB'S LADDER
Polemonium reptans
Phlox Family (Polemoniaceae)

Description: The leaves are made up of 8–10 lanceolate leaflets and alternate on the stem of this 6–18" plant. The ½–¾" flowers have 5 light blue petals that form a bell.

Bloom Season: April–June

Habitat/Range: In moist wooded areas from New York to Minnesota and south to Georgia and Oklahoma. Mostly in the mountains.

Comments: *Polemonium reptans* is a midwestern and southern species that is cultivated in northeastern gardens. A similar plant, also called Jacob's Ladder *(Polemonium van-bruntiae),* is native to the mountains in the northeast. The 2 plants look very much alike and differ only in the length of the stamens, which protrude far beyond its petals in *Polemonium van-bruntiae.*

Asiatic Dayflower

ASIATIC DAYFLOWER
Commelina communis
Pickerelweed Family (Pontederiaceae)

Description: The lanceolate, entire leaves alternate on the stem of this 6–12" plant. The ½–1" flowers have 2 blue petals opposite each other and 1 petal that forms a small white lip. The yellow stamens are prominently displayed.

Bloom Season: June–October

Habitat/Range: On roadsides, beside trails, and in waste places from Massachusetts to Wisconsin and Nebraska and south to Georgia.

Comments: This dayflower is from Asia and is another plant that propagates easily and has become a pest in many places. It is easy to find the plant throughout the Southern Appalachian Mountains. The Virginia Dayflower *(Commelina virginica)* also grows in the Southern Appalachian Mountains but is much harder to find. It looks much like the Asiatic Dayflower, but all 3 petals are blue.

BLUETS OR QUAKER LADIES
Houstonia caerulea
Madder Family (Rubiaceae)

Description: The short, lanceolate, entire leaves are opposite on the stem of this 2–8" plant. The ½" flowers have 4 blue or white petals and a yellow center.

Bloom Season: April–June

Habitat/Range: In open, grassy places or on wet rocks from Nova Scotia to Georgia and Arkansas.

Comments: This common plant often grows in tufts along the side of the Appalachian Trail. It is also found in Fort Desoto State Park, Alabama. Also called Innocence, this small plant has several other names in English.

Bluets or Quaker Ladies

LARGE HOUSTONIA
Houstonia purpurea
Madder Family (Rubiaceae)

Description: The lanceolate leaves are oppo-site each other on the stem of this 4–16" plant. The leaves have 3–5 veins. The ¼" flowers are light blue or white and in the form of a cup with 4 flared petals.

Bloom Season: April–September

Habitat/Range: At the edges of trails and roads, especially in the mountains from Mary-land to Iowa and south to Kentucky and Alabama.

Comments: The delicate flowers of this pretty little plant stick around after the lush displays of the early spring woods are gone. Small and light colored, they can easily be overlooked by hikers on woodland trails.

Large Houstonia

Blue Toadflax

BLUE TOADFLAX
Linaria canadensis
Snapdragon Family (Scrophulariaceae)

Description: The narrow, entire leaves alter-nate on the stem of this 4–24" plant. The ¼" flowers have 5 blue petals and a white center and grow at the top of slender stems.

Bloom Season: May–September

Habitat/Range: In dry soils from Nova Sco-tia west to Minnesota and Oregon and south to Florida and Texas.

Comments: Also called Old Field Toadflax because it tends to grow in large colonies in old fields. It can be viewed in Georgia at the Sosebee Cove area of Chattahoochee National Forest and at Talullah Gorge State Park. Often a circle of runners grows from the base of the plant.

GREEN AND BROWN FLOWERS

Common Cattail

Poison Ivy

POISON IVY
Toxicodendron radicans
Sumac Family (Anacardiaceae)

Description: The leaves of Poison Ivy can vary in shape. Sometimes they are toothed ovals. Sometimes they can look like small oak leaves. The leaves are always in a group of 3 on the stem of this vine. When the leaves are young, they are often shiny and reddish. As the vine matures, the leaves turn green, and in moist locations with a long growing season, the leaves can be very large. The vine is covered with hairs. The tiny flowers have 5 greenish white petals and grow in a cluster.

Bloom Season: May–June

Habitat/Range: In trees and thickets and along fences from Nova Scotia to British Columbia and south to Florida and Texas.

Comments: All parts of the plant are poisonous, and contact with any part of the plant can cause severe, weeping rashes on people who are sensitive to the irritant in the oil of the plant. The vine is deciduous but can be identified in winter because the thick stem is extremely hairy. Some books separate the Poison Ivy vine with oak-shaped leaves into a separate plant they call Poison Oak *(Toxicodendron toxicarium)*. Whatever it is called, both plants have the same properties and should be avoided.

Wild Ginger

WILD GINGER
Asarum canadense
Birthwort Family (Aristolochiaceae)

Description: The 2 heart-shaped leaves are at the base of this 6–9" plant. The 1" purple or brown flowers have 3 pointed lobes. The flowers are found at the base of the plant and are usually hidden by the leaves.

Bloom Season: April–June

Habitat/Range: In rich woods from New Brunswick to Manitoba and south to North Carolina and Kansas.

Comments: Native Americans used the root of the plant as a flavoring for food. The early colonists adopted it as a replacement for the ginger they had used in Europe, hence it came to be known as Wild Ginger. The ginger now used in cooking is a native of Asia. Wild Ginger will grow anywhere there is a small amount of rich soil and a source of water.

BLUE COHOSH OR PAPOOSE-ROOT
Caulophyllum thalictroides
Barberry Family (Berberidaceae)

Description: The leaves, divided into 3 toothed leaflets, form whorls on the stem of this 1–3' plant. The ½" flowers have 6 greenish or purple petals.

Bloom Season: April–June

Habitat/Range: In woods from New Brunswick to Georgia.

Comments: Blue Cohosh can easily be overlooked in the woods of Fort Desoto State Park in Alabama or in the Sosebee Cove area of the Chattahoochee National Forest in Georgia. The plant is tall and the flowers are a subtle greenish brown. When it blooms in mid-April, everyone is looking near the ground to see wonderful, eye-catching trillium and lady's slippers blooming. The name Papoose-Root comes about because Native Americans used the roots to ease childbirth.

Blue Cohosh or Papoose-Root

Indian Cucumber Root

INDIAN CUCUMBER ROOT
Medeola virginiana
Lily Family (Lilliaceae)

Description: The lanceolate, entire leaves form 2 whorls on the stem of this 1–3' plant. The ¼" flowers usually hang down under the top whorl of 3–5 leaves. The 2 flowers, 1 on each side of the stem, have 6 greenish purple petals in the shape of a dangling bell.

Bloom Season: April–July

Habitat/Range: In moist woods and thickets from Nova Scotia to Ontario and south to Tennessee and Florida.

Comments: The mystery of this plant is why it is called Cucumber Root. The root of the plant is white and looks something like a small parsnip or a white carrot. The root was usually eaten raw and is often peppery. Indian Cucumber Root blooms in mid-April along the nature trail at Fort Mountain State Park, Georgia.

ALUMROOT
Heuchera americana
Saxifrage Family (Saxifragaceae)

Description: The lobed leaves are at the base of this 1–3' plant. The tiny, greenish purple flowers are in clusters on the top of a long stem that is separate from the rosette of leaves. Each flower has 5 petals and the stamens protrude.

Bloom Season: April–June

Habitat/Range: In mountainous areas from Virginia south to Georgia, and as far north as Connecticut and Ohio in rocky, shaded areas of the Coastal Plain and the Piedmont.

Comments: The plant grows from an underground stem *(rhizome)*. The common name refers to the rhizome having an astringent quality. The plant can be found along the Blue Ridge Parkway and along the Chestnut Hill Trail in Great Smoky Mountains National Park.

Alumroot

COMMON CATTAIL
Typha latifolia
Cattail Family (Typhaceae)

Description: The large, grasslike, entire leaves alternate on the stem of this 4–8' plant. The brown flowers form a 4–8", dense, cylindrical spike. The 2 portions of the flower cluster touch each other.

Bloom Season: May–July

Habitat/Range: In wet places and marshes throughout North America, except in the extreme North.

Comments: Narrow-Leaved Cattail *(Typha angustifolia)* also grows in the Southern Appalachians. Its 2 portions of the flower are separated. In both cattails the upper half of the spike has male flowers and the lower half of the spike contains female flowers. Native Americans dried and ground the roots of cattail into a meal and peeled and ate the young shoots.

Common Cattail

Great Angelica

GREAT ANGELICA
Angelica atropurpurea
Parsley Family (Umbelliferae)

Description: The large, divided leaves alternate on the stem of this 4–10' plant. The tiny flowers have 5 greenish white petals and form a large, roundish cluster.

Bloom Season: May–September

Habitat/Range: In moist places and swamps from Labrador to Minnesota and south to North Carolina.

Comments: Many members of the parsley family are similar in appearance and very poisonous. Unless you are certain of the identification of a plant, it is best to leave all members of this family alone. Great Angelica can be found in meadows off the Blue Ridge Parkway around mile 293 in North Carolina.

Wood Nettle

WOOD NETTLE
Laportea canadensis
Nettle Family (Urticaceae)

Description: The ovate, toothed leaves are on long stalks and alternate on the stem of this 3–6" plant. The tiny, greenish flowers grow mostly in the axil of the leaves and form a long cluster.

Bloom Season: June–August

Habitat/Range: In rich woods from Nova Scotia to North Dakota and south to Florida and Kansas.

Comments: This is a common plant of Southern Appalachian woods, and it is a good plant to be able to recognize. It is not pretty, but its bristly hairs can sting if brushed against and leave a very unpleasant sensation for many minutes. It grows in the Cascade Recreation Area of Jefferson National Forest, Virginia, and on the Chimney Top Nature Trail in Great Smoky Mountains National Park.

$\mathscr{P}$LACES CITED

These are places where we have seen the flowers cited in the book. They are not places where the plants grow exclusively, since many of these plants can be seen in many other locations throughout the Southern Appalachians and the United States.

ALABAMA

Desoto State Park

Location: This more than 5,000-acre park situated along the Little River is in northeastern Alabama, 8 miles northeast of Fort Payne.

Additional Information:
Desoto State Park Office
13883 County Road 89
Fort Payne, AL 35967
(256) 845–0051
(800) 568–8840
www.dcnr.state.al.us

GEORGIA

Chattahoochee National Forest

Location: The Chattahoochee National Forest consists of about 750,000 acres located in northern Georgia at the borders with Tennessee and North Carolina.

Additional Information:
Forest Supervisor
U.S. Forest Service
508 Oak Street N.W.
Gainesville, GA 30501
(770) 297–3000
www.fs.fed.us/conf

Fort Mountain State Park

Location: This 3,500-acre park is in northern Georgia, 8 miles east of Chatsworth.

Additional Information:
Fort Mountain State Park
181 Fort Mountain Park Road
Chatsworth, GA 30705
(706) 695–2621
www.gastateparks.org

James H. "Sloppy" Floyd Park

Location: Located in northwestern Georgia, this park is 3 miles southeast of Summerville.

Additional Information:
James H. "Sloppy" Floyd Park
Route 1, Box 291
Summerville, GA 30747
(706) 857–0826
www.gastateparks.org

Tallulah Gorge State Park

Location: This park is located in northern Georgia in the town of Tallulah Falls.

Additional Information:
Georgia State Parks and Historic Sites
205 Butler Street S.E.
Atlanta, GA 30334
(404) 656–2720
www.gastateparks.org

NORTH CAROLINA

Blue Ridge Parkway

Location: This 470-mile-long scenic parkway follows the crest of the Southern Appalachians connecting Shenandoah National Park in the north with Great Smoky Mountains National Park to the south. It runs from Virginia south to North Carolina.

Additional Information:
National Park Service
U.S. Department of the Interior
700 Northwestern Bank Building
Asheville, NC 28801
www.nps.gov

Great Smoky Mountains National Park

Location: Located where Tennessee meets North Carolina; the park is in both states.

Additional Information:
Superintendent, Great Smoky Mountains National Park
107 Park Headquarters Road
Gatlinburg, TN 37738
(865) 436–1200
www.nps.gov/grsm

Nantahala National Forest

Location: This park is located in the southwestern tip of North Carolina.

Additional Information:
U.S. Forest Service
P. O. Box 2750
Asheville, NC 28802
(704) 257–4200
www.fs.fed.us

TENNESSEE

Great Smoky Mountains National Park

Location: This park is located in eastern Tennessee at the border with North Carolina. It is situated in both states.

Additional Information:
Superintendent, Great Smoky Mountains National Park
107 Park Headquarters Road
Gatlinburg, TN 37738
(865) 436–1200
www.nps.gov/grsm

VIRGINIA

Blue Ridge Parkway

Location: This is a scenic parkway running 470 miles along the crest of the Southern Appalachians from the southern terminus of Shenandoah National Park and the George Washington National Forest to the Great Smoky Mountains National Park to the south. It runs from Virginia south to North Carolina.

Additional Information:
National Park Service
U.S. Department of the Interior
700 Northwestern Bank Building
Asheville, NC 28801
www.nps.gov

George Washington and Jefferson National Forests

Location: These two forests stretch approximately north-south along the Appalachians in Virginia. The Blue Ridge Parkway runs through part of the George Washington National Forest south of Shenandoah National Park. The Jefferson National Forest is south of this and both forests also include a large area west of the Blue Ridge Parkway.

Additional Information:
National Forest Recreation
Supervisor's Office
5162 Valleypointe Parkway
Roanoke, VA 24019
(540) 265–5100
www.fs.fed.us/gwjnf

Hungry Mother State Park

Location: This park is located outside the town of Marion, Virginia.

Additional Information:
Hungry Mother State Park
2854 Park Boulevard
Marion, VA 24354
(540) 781–7400
www.state.va.us/~dcr

WEST VIRGINIA

New River Gorge National River

Location: Located in southern West Virginia, this park has 70,000 acres of land along the New River between Hinton and Fayetteville.

Additional Information:
New River Gorge National River
Park Headquarters
P.O. Box 246
Glen Jean, WV 25846
(304) 465–0508
www.nps.gov/neri

OTHER PLACES

There are some other places where a large variety of wildflowers may be seen. These are not parks and trails for hiking, but rather preserves where plants from many parts of the country are grown. They are a form of living museum.

Bowman's Hill Wildflower Preserve

Bowman's Hill Wildflower Preserve's 100 acres are administered by the Bowman's Hill Wildflower Preserve Association in cooperation with the Pennsylvania Historical and Museum Commission. The wildflowers grow on labeled trails and roads.

Location: Located in southeastern Pennsylvania outside the town of New Hope, Pennsylvania.

Additional Information:
Bowman's Hill Wildflower Preserve
P.O. Box 685
New Hope, PA 18938
(215) 862–2924
www.bhwp.org

U.S. National Arboretum

The arboretum is an Agricultural Research Service education and research facility with educational programs, germ-plasm conservation facilities, and display gardens. Wildflowers from around the country are cultivated in Fern Valley.

Location: Located in northeast Washington, D.C.

Additional Information:
U.S. National Arboretum
3501 New York Avenue, N.E.
Washington, D.C. 20002-2726
(202) 245–4575
www.ars-grin.gov/ars/beltsville/na

FOR MORE INFORMATION

Park and Forest Agencies Web Sites

United States

National Parks: www.nps.gov
National Forests: www.fs.fed.us

State Government Agencies

Alabama State Parks and Forests:
www.dcnr.state.al.us

Georgia State Parks: www.ganet.org/dnr
Georgia State Forests: www.gfc.state.ga.us

North Carolina State Parks:
www.enr.state.nc.us/files/division.htm

Tennessee State Parks & Natural Areas:
www.state.tn.us/environment/

Virginia State Forests:
state.vipnet.org/dof/stforest/stforest.htm
Virginia State Parks:
www.dcr.state.va.us/parks/

West Virginia State Parks and Forests:
www.dnr.state.wv.us

ADDITIONAL READING

Adams, Kevin, and Marty Casstevens. *Wildflowers of the Southern Appalachians: How to Photograph and Identify Them.* Winston Salem, NC: John F. Blair, 1996.

A guide to identifying and photographing wildflowers of the Southern Appalachians.

Brill, Steve, and Evelyn Dean. *Identifying and Harvesting Edible and Medicinal Plants in Wild (and Not So Wild) Places.* New York: Hearst Books, 1994.

A guide to finding wild plants and using them for food and medicine.

Britton, Nathaniel Lord, and Addison Brown. *An Illustrated Flora of the Northern United States and Canada, Volumes I, II, and III.* New York: Dover Publications, Inc., 1970.

A comprehensive work in three volumes on the flora of the northeastern United States and adjacent Canada.

Coffey, Timothy. *The History and Folklore of North American Wildflowers.* Boston and New York: Houghton Mifflin Company, 1993.

The place of hundreds of plants in folklore, history, and social custom, and as foods and medicines.

Cox, W. Eugene. *Great Smoky Mountains: The Story Behind the Scenery.* Las Vegas, NV: KC Publications, 1998.

A summary of facts, figures, and pictures of the Great Smoky Mountains.

Densmore, Frances. *How Indians Use Wild Plants for Food, Medicine, and Crafts.* New York: Dover Publication, Inc., 1974.

This is a republication of a much earlier paper, "Uses of Plants by the Chippewa Indians" in a report of the Bureau of American Ethnology to the Smithsonian Institution.

Foster, Steven, and James Duke. *Eastern and Central Medicinal Plants.* Boston and New York: Peterson Field Guides, Houghton Mifflin Company., 1990.

A survey of 500 medicinal herbs and plants growing in eastern and central North America.

Foster, Steven and Roger C. Caras. *Venomous Animals and Poisonous Plants.* Boston and New York: Peterson Field Guides, Houghton Mifflin Company, 1994.

A field guide to wildflowers, trees, and shrubs that can cause toxic reactions.

Gray, Asa. *Gray's Manual of Botany,* 8th ed. New York: American Book Co., 1950.

The 1950 edition of this book on flowering plants and ferns of the central and northeastern United States was largely rewritten by Merritt Lyndon Fernall, Professor Emeritus and former Director of Gray Herbarium at Harvard.

Hutson, Robert W., William F. Hutson, and Aaron J. Sharp. *Campbell, Hutson, and Sharp's Great Smoky Mountains Wildflowers.* Northbrook IL: Windy Pines Publishing, 1995.

A guide to some of the wildflowers in the Great Smoky Mountains.

Jones, Pamela A. *Just Weeds: History, Myths, and Uses.* Shelburne, VT: Chapters Publishing Ltd., 1994.

Descriptions of 30 "weeds" or wild plants, where they grow, and how they have been used by humans.

Justice, William S., and C. Ritchie Bell. *Wild Flowers of North Carolina.* Chapel Hill, North Carolina: University of North Carolina Press, 1968.

A guide to wildflowers found in North Carolina.

Lawrence, Susannah and Barbara Gross. *The Audubon Society Field Guide to the Natural Places of the Mid-Atlantic States: Inland.* New York: Pantheon Books, 1984.

Tours through inland natural sites of the mid-Atlantic states.

Meyer, Joseph E., revised and enlarged by C. Meyer. *The Herbalist.* Glenwood, IL: Meyerbooks, 1993.

A collection of plants that have been used for medicine, food, dyes, scents, and spices.

Millspaugh, Charles F. *American Medicinal Plants.* New York: Dover Publications, Inc., 1974.

This republication of a book originally published in 1892 lists the uses of plants and their chemical characteristics in treating over 1,000 ailments. Although many of these treatments are now considered questionable, the publication is of historical interest.

Newcomb, Lawrence. *Newcomb's Wildflower Guide.* Boston, Toronto, London: Little, Brown and Company, 1974.

This popular guide uses line drawings to illustrate wildflowers from eastern Canada through Ontario and south to northern North Carolina and Tennessee.

Peterson, Roger Tory, and Margaret McKenny. *Wildflowers Northeastern/North-Central North America.* Boston: Houghton Mifflin Company, 1968.

A line-drawing illustrated field guide for the identification of wildflowers with explanatory text.

Rickett, Harold William, *Wildflowers of the United States, Volume One: Parts I and II; The Northeastern States, 1965,* New York: McGraw-Hill Book Company.

A now out-of-print publication of the New York Botanical Garden with the wildflowers of the northeastern United States.

Roberts, David C. *Geology of Eastern North America.* Boston and New York: Peterson Field Guides, Houghton Mifflin Company, 1996.

This book explores eastern North America's geological features as well as geological theories of the processes that took place over millions of years leading to their present configuration.

Saunders, Charles Francis. *Edible and Useful Plants of the U.S. and Canada.* New York: Dover Publications, Inc., 1976.

This republication of a 1934 edition discusses edible and useful wild plants in the United States.

Smith, Richard M. *Wildflowers of the Southern Mountains.* Knoxville, TN: University of Tennessee Press, 1998.

This field guide covers wildflowers growing in the southern mountains.

Wheelwright, Edith Grey. *Medicinal Plants and Their History.* New York: Dover Publications, 1974.

A republication of a 1935 edition reviewing the history of herbs and plants in medicine.

GLOSSARY

alternate: A pattern of leaves growing singly at each node of the stem and not opposite each other.

axil: The point at which the leaf joins the stem.

basal: The leaves growing from the bottom of the plant.

bract: A leaflike structure different from the foliage leaves, often at the point where the flower emerges.

calyx: The outermost flower parts. All the sepals together form the calyx.

cleft: A leaf with a deep cut, sometimes to the midrib of the leaf, is described as cleft.

corm: An underground part of stem, like a bulb, whose function is food storage or reproduction.

corolla: The petals all together are called the corolla; the upper, colored, portion being the petals.

disk: The center part of composite flowers like the daisy.

divided: A leaf cut one or more times, possibly all the way to the middle of the leaf, is said to be divided.

entire: A leaf is characterized as entire if the outside margin of the leaf is continuous and unbroken.

fernlike: Leaves that somewhat resemble the leaves of a fern.

head: The dense, short, flowering portion of a plant.

lanceolate: A leaf much longer than it is wide, tapered toward the tip, and widest below the middle.

leaflet: One segment of a compound leaf having several parts.

lips: Sometimes petals appear in an upper and lower configuration called lips, as in orchids or violets.

lobed: Leaves cut but not so deeply as to reach the midrib are lobed.

midrib: The middle vein of a leaf or leaflet.

native: Plants that grow in a region not introduced by humans.

naturalized: Plants that have escaped cultivation or been introduced by humans into an area but do not take over and displace the native vegetation.

ovary: Produces the seeds, located at the base of the pistil.

pistil: The reproductive organ of the flower (containing the style, ovary, and stigma).

ray: The flat, petal-like flowers that circle the disk flowers of a composite.

reflexed: Bent backward sharply.

regular: Most flowers are regular, with petals arranged in a symmetrical pattern and each petal similar to all the others in shape and color, as in the daisy.

rhizome: The stem below the earth, with nodes that produce roots.

rootstock: A below-ground stem.

sepal: the lower part of the flower, below the petals, usually green.

sheath: A structure, possibly tubular, surrounding another part of the plant.

spadix: A stalk in the shape of a club where many tiny blossoms grow.

spathe: A partial, hoodlike covering over the spadix.

spike: A long, leafless stem bearing the flower.

spur: A tubular extension of a flower.

stalk: The portion of the plant attaching a leaf or flower to the stem.

stamen: The portion of the flower bearing pollen.

stem: The main portion of a plant on which grow the leaves and flower.

stem leaves: These grow above the plant base. A plant can have both basal and stem leaves.

stigma: The tip of the pistil that receives pollen.

style: The narrow stalk of the reproductive organ, or pistil.

tendril: A slender part of a stem or leaf whose purpose is to support the plant.

toothed: A part of the plant with a sawtooth edge.

umbel: A growth pattern in which flowers appear in an umbrella shape.

wing: A thin flap at the edge of a leafstalk or along a stem or other part of the plant.

whorl: Leaves growing in a circling arrangement around the stem of the plant are in a whorl.

$\mathcal{I}$NDEX

ABOUT THE AUTHORS

Barbara and Victor Medina are a husband and wife team that has spent several decades rambling through the meadows, woods, and bogs in search of wildflowers. Their searches have taken them from well-known national parks to small ecological gems off the beaten path. They have photographed and cataloged more than 800 wildflowers in the process. They are members of the Maryland Native Plant Society, the Sierra Club, the Appalachian Mountain Club, and the Nature Conservancy.

Barbara Medina has had a one-woman show of her wildflower photographs at the National Arboretum in Washington, D.C. She is the founder and was the first president of the Maryland Native Plant Society. She leads wildflower walks for schools, colleges, and environmental organizations, as well as for the Smithsonian Institution Associates program in Washington, D.C.

Victor Medina has had varied careers as an inventor, research chemist, and director of research administration at major universities. He holds several patents, has served as a book reviewer for special publications within the field of research administration, and was a contributing author for a book on fuel cell chemistry. He is currently the editor of a community newsletter.